AN UPHILL ROAD IN INDIA

AN UPHILL ROAD IN INDIA

M. L. CHRISTLIEB

GYAN

Published by

GYAN

Gyan Publishing House
5, Ansari Road
Daryaganj, New Delhi-110002
Phone: 011-47034999, 9811692060
E-mail: books@gyanbooks.com

Distribution Network
gyanbooks.com
India, USA, Canada, UK, Australia

ISBN: 978-93-7097-469-2 (PB)

First Published, 1928

2nd Impression 2025

Printed at: Gyan Press, Delhi.

AN UPHILL ROAD IN INDIA
Arthur M. L. CHRISTLIEB

AN UPHILL ROAD IN INDIA

AN UPHILL ROAD IN INDIA

BY

M. L. CHRISTLIEB

"*And does the road wind uphill all the way?*
Yes, to the very end."
C. Rossetti

BOSTON AND NEW YORK
HOUGHTON MIFFLIN COMPANY
1928

TO

E.

THE LIFELONG FRIEND

WHOSE LOVE AND SYMPATHY

PRESERVED THE LETTERS FROM WHICH

THESE PAGES ARE TAKEN

FOREWORD

The following pages—as the dedication conveys—are collected from a correspondence covering a period of over twenty years. The friend to whom it was addressed shared the first period of service in India with the writer; of the beginning of their missionary work there is, therefore, no detailed record. The letters begin when the writer returned to India alone.

As they contained a great deal of merely personal interest some editing had to be done, also a few additions made here and there, as the public at home could not be counted upon to possess the same knowledge of India as the recipient of the letters. For the sake of clearness in presenting some phase of work absolute chronology could not be observed in the sequence of chapters. All incidents, conversations, etc., are descriptions of current happenings.

The names of most places and of persons still living have been changed.

The book does not pretend to be a presentment of new facts concerning India; it is but a simple human recital of daily experiences among a much-loved Eastern people. Should it help to provoke anyone to spend thought upon the great dependency to which we are so closely bound it would be great reward.

M. L. CHRISTLIEB.

OXFORD, 1927.

An Uphill Road in India

CHAPTER I

Late at night the train drew up at the familiar little country station. Lanterns moved up and down the dark platform. I could hear Dorcas's voice and Chidananda's, and what a hearty welcome followed when we found one another! But the twenty-eight hours' railway journey from Bombay through the hot Deccan had, somehow, been so tiring that everything felt dismal. Or was it the first taste of having no companion at Andapur?

Erana the faithful was in attendance at the bungalow; he had risen to a jug of cocoa which looked forlorn on the big dining-table; presently an even more forlorn bazaar loar made its appearance; I unpacked some cheese bought at Bombay and partook of supper—though the loneliness almost overcame me.

* * * * *

Potukonda. I am on a round of visits to our out-stations and am writing in my tent. It is delightful to be again in camp, though it has certainly a few drawbacks; the tent walls are black with mosquitoes, but they will, for the most part, sit still till sundown. Through the holes in the tent mat cattle ticks keep on coming up; I have taken them off my legs three at a time, and if I look I can always see nine or ten crawling on the floor—evidently the cattle like the shade of these trees as much as I do—and the ground is full of these pests. The plague of the tiny red ants is also abroad, they are here in millions, on my bed, on me, everywhere. I keep on killing them as I write. Yet I love this tent life, it is delicious to be treading on Mother Earth, though the tree roots hidden by the mat nearly upset my balance; I like to hear the branches rustling where the flying foxes hang themselves up at night, and the screech-owls let forth like a banshee; I like to see the air quivering over the ground at noon, and to hear the field of tall *cholum* stalks respond to the wind with a sound as of many waters. I like to see the great stretches of grey plains beyond, and villagers passing to and fro. I like to hear the call of the herd boys to their goats and their cattle, and to see the coolie women come past at sundown with their baskets of garnered cotton or corn and to chat with them; we are all friendly wayfarers here.

And above all I like to be back in the villages themselves. Early to-day Bhagyamma and I were in the house of a Sudra widow who is struggling to bring up five children. Our talk was perpetually interrupted by beggars coming round with their tinkling bells and recitations. One was proudly walking under an English umbrella, clothes upon clothes were hanging round his shoulders; there he stood looking sleek, chanting and holding out his bowl to the poor widow who with her children has to fast often enough! The very next minute came another, father and son; the boy held the sacred trident of Vishnu with a lime stuck on each prong; the father seemed a harmless rustic, though the trident marked on his forehead gave him a fierce appearance. Akkamma got up again to get the handful of grain; for not to give is sin, and giving certainly causes merit to accrue to the bestower.

My Western patience snapped. "Is it not evil of thee, oh beggar of many clothes and with much grain in thy bowl," I addressed him, "to come asking of this widow who has naught? Why dost thou not work for a living even as she does?"

"No work was ever taught me but this," replied the beggar stolidly.

"Would it not be well to teach thy son, or send him to be taught, some work?"

"It is not our custom. This is our fate." Rather pityingly he looked at me and my ignorance; Akkamma too, seemed to think there were more things under the sun than a Westerner understood! India has no poor law, no poor rates, no charity organization society, and prides herself on these facts; but are the innumerable mendicants battening on the community an improvement? In that half-hour with Akkamma I counted five, and to all she gave. I further discovered that those five children she slaves for are not her own, but those of a concubine her husband kept; they were left deserted and she is shouldering the whole burden. I bow to that village woman and her obedience to spiritual laws as far as she knows them.

But my rejoicing was blurred by the next experience. We walked past a little private school. The schoolmaster came out to greet us. He was a Brahmin; but the woman introduced presently as his wife gave me the impression of a different caste. As castes cannot intermarry, this must be an irregular household, I thought, and it was even so. This woman was the daughter of another irregular household; her father, a goldsmith, is an old acquaintance of ours who always asks for a visit. That there is any discrepancy between his interest in religion and his domestic conduct does not seem to occur to him. Nor to anyone. The caste people in this village send their sons to the house of the Brahmin and the goldsmith's daughter. No doubt the very children understand the relationship. Public callousness towards these things seems to me utterly appalling. Yes, there are deplorable conditions at home; but would public opinion anywhere be as indifferent as in this village with regard to those to whom the teaching of the young is entrusted?

The calls to visit houses were many. The lives of women in the villages are often dull; the advent of a white woman is an event. It gets reported that "our words come to her"; naturally the wish arises to see and hear this strange apparition. But when all allowance is made for this the signs of hunger of another kind may be discerned too.

They are sheep without a shepherd. Hinduism is a religion that has attained great spiritual heights and discerned some truths with great insight; but it takes no pains to make these accessible to the ignorant. The common people have to find their way through the difficult maze of this life of ours, untaught save by family and village ceremonies inculcating chiefly the fear of demons; they cannot read, they have no education of any kind. There are temples, but no service in our sense is ever held there; it is a sanctuary for placing offerings and reciting prayers. Occasionally indeed religious teachers come round; but as regards the latter the proverb has arisen, "*bôdha guru, bâdha guru*"—"not teachers, tormentors"—i.e. demanding substantial offerings; and with the power to curse and even outcaste they have the whip hand! So their visits are not occasions of unmixed joy to the villagers.

On return I found my carts standing loaded and ready to start under the tamarind-trees, but also Jeshaya, one of our Christian *Malas*.[1] With a family grouped around him he made a fluent appeal from which there was no escape.

"See these seven children! I cannot feed them—behold Arôgyam, behold Jivi, you must take them! I throw them on you, they are your affair; do what you like; they are not mine but yours; take them and educate them; you are their father and mother . . ." an unending stream.

"Don't you think it very unjust," I got in at last, "when you have married of your own free will to throw your family cares on me who have refused marriage?"

The Biblewoman behind me tittered; but no sense of humour or pity moved Jeshaya who went on pleading unperturbed.

[1] The name of a Telugu low-caste section.

"Well, my last word," I said, hard driven. "I will try and get Arôgyam into the Boarding School, but Jivi must wait, and you must pay the fees."

I drove off, seated in state on my tent bundles in the uncovered cart; the village children running behind and before and beside, the women staring, the Christians salaaming, the dogs barking, my mind revolving all the way round the problem of a Boarding Home in our own district instead of only one a hundred miles away. Girls get thrown at one's head, so to speak. But accommodation for them, finance, matron, teachers—what formidable mountains! not to speak of Committees out here *and* Boards at home. Also, it will tie one to headquarters. What about the villages?

Thus cogitating I jogged on to Munti, where I climbed down to see the little new school building; all the villagers came round, such noise, dust, dirt, smells! The sun was sinking, the cattle were coming home in great herds, and all the *Mala* people seemed to lift their voices not with one accord but rather many discords, and this was their cry, "We are poor, it is cold at night, give our children a jacket!" Thus pleading they followed us a long way as we walked on into the gathering shadows. Under the spreading banyan-tree two miles farther on we camped for the night. I sat in the starlight and thought over the many problems encountered in this one day, the last perhaps the chief, our Christian *Malas* and their poverty; Christianity spreading among a class economically dependent on caste people who are hostile to their adoption of Christianity; what is to be done? Attack the caste people?

It seemed a formidable undertaking; there are too many of them; but has not Christianity always attempted the impossible?

Next morning Bhagyamma and I were up before the sun and away to a caste village. The path led through fields; white softness was bursting from the brown cotton pods ready for reaping; castor oil plants spread broad leaves in the sun; in *cholum* fields the tall stalks, their cobs already reaped, stood waving in the breeze. " He walked through the cornfields on the Sabbath day " floated into my mind. Why, this was Sunday too!

" He went about among the towns and villages of Galilee." If He would only come and walk among the towns and villages of India! What can *we* do ? Often I feel horribly incompetent. The effort to begin a talk with the people has not yet become easier. Realizing their atmosphere better than before, one realizes also much better the greatness of the difficulty of adapting oneself to it. I am ashamed to confess that I find myself face to face with the old temptation to shirk the effort of breaking through barriers. " What shall I say when I get to the village ? " is apt to remain a nervous and uncomfortable meditation on the way there.

This morning we accomplished one small thing. In a well-to-do farmer's house there is a sick wife; as she has no children, the husband is utterly indifferent. He keeps another establishment down the same street; of course everyone knows it. For long she had been eager to go to our Mission hospital. But whenever the husband's permission was asked he said callously, " You can die. I don't want you. You have no son." To-day we found him in and Bhagyamma attacked him. In glowing terms she described my grandeur and influence, my sorrow at his wife's state, the condescension of promising a letter which should smooth all things for them at the hospital—the danger of arousing my anger—the man wilted. " I will take her to hospital myself."

So far so good! It propped up my self-respect, which presently had to suffer some shocks. In one house a woman regarded me earnestly. Was she thinking about what I was saying ?

" Do you often bathe ? " she interrupted, evidently unable to contain herself. " Your hair looks very dirty."

Poor Bhagyamma nearly had a fit. I had taken my sun

topee off, and so it was revealed that my hair lay not in well-oiled flatness on my skull, but stood off in unpleasing independence. Shall I, must I, take to coco-nut oil? There are heights I cannot reach. I am willing to be parted from my nearest and dearest, to be alone in the wide Indian plains and trudge to villages, to tussle with strange tongues and strange people, and any other little thing like that, but I cannot, will not, put coco-nut oil with its penetrating and rancid smell on my hair!

Meanwhile another woman, taking courage, was fingering my skirt. "Cotton," she remarked. I became acutely aware that the best people in India wear silk. The woman was examining all garments within reach.

"She wears three *saris*," she announced to the company in pained astonishment. They looked their amazement.

"It is our custom," I pleaded. Custom, of course, is sacred for all; they nodded understandingly. "Yes, you have yours, and we have ours."

Frankness became the order of the meeting. "How old do you think she is?" the audience began speculating to one another, while Bhagyamma endeavoured in vain to lead them back to piety. A man had strolled in at the court-yard and overheard the question.

"Twenty-four," he asserted.

I confessed to more.

"Forty," said a woman promptly, rousing my indignation. Another woman now looked at me searchingly.

"Please, you are very wise, you know everything, will you tell me one thing?"

Was she going to ask a question about religion?

"Please tell me something to stop my hair turning grey."

* * * * *

But we met more than that this morning. In another family a young woman sat apart from others; I noticed her nose was half gone. "Is she a relative?" I asked the women.

Shoulders were shrugged and glances directed at neighbouring houses, as if she must have strayed in from somewhere. I gathered that she did not belong to that household, and was meant to gather that. But the fact is that after the girl's own husband deserted her in childhood the son of this house became her protector; her children count as his sons, he married no other woman. Then came illness and disfigurement. They are ashamed of her, and if asked who she is the evasive reply is, "Who can she be?" She looked at me with sad eyes; should they choose they can turn her out; she has no redress and would have no refuge. Could we have a Home for such women?

Almost the next moment my thoughts along these lines were confirmed. Down the street a girl came limping, both her feet were turned inward and crippled. She had a pretty face and was not more than perhaps seventeen years of age.

"That is Achita," said Bhagyamma, following my look.

"Let us go to her house," I suggested, "as you know her."

The father and mother were both at home, and what do you think they mean to do with their only daughter? Seeing no chance of a suitable marriage they have destined her for a bad life.

"What can we do?" they said. "Who would marry her? We are not rich enough to buy a son-in-law for a crippled girl."

"But the girl is now listening to me," said Bhagyamma afterwards, "and she utterly refuses that life."

Will she be strong enough to resist pressure as the years go on?

We certainly need a Home for girls and women for whom Hinduism has no use and no protection.

CHAPTER II

Bukkuru. It is the evening of New Year's Day, begun in a strange and fateful way.

Jeanie Hamilton who had come to help us celebrate Christmas in lonely Andapur, wanted to see something of our district. Two days ago we came to this out-station. George Pillay, the Christian doctor here, was delighted. I think sometimes it frets him that Christianity is not thought much of in this town; he would like it to make a better show. Therefore we two, arriving just at this season, might be regarded as heaven-sent lions, an opportunity not to be wasted for a New Year's *tamasha* which should impress Hindu society with Christian grandeur. I do not mean there was no evangelistic zeal—there probably was, but a bit mixed.

All round the town he went and invited its *élite* to an evening meeting; the Magistrate, the *Karnam*,[1] everybody of any standing; he also engaged the town band and arranged for torches and decorations. Last of all he came to us.

"You will be called for by the band at 6 p.m.; and we will go in procession through the town."

The prospect of a band deafening with tomtoms, drums, and flutes was not alluring, nor marching in the midst of a crowd, and we frankly avowed our preferences for a quieter mode of procedure.

"Oh, my lions," said the disappointed medico, "please roar. I entreat that you will roar." That, in substance, was his—much prolonged—peroration.

Comprehending that unless we agreed to roar he would sit there and go on entreating us very likely till the band arrived, we economized by consenting at once.

[1] Government official in charge of land and land records.

"And we shall all speak about the same text; you and I and the Catechist, ten minutes each: 'teach me to know the number of my days, that I may apply my heart unto wisdom.'"

Evening arrived, and the band, and the torches, and the crowd. The band tuned up, and shrilled, and banged; the torches flared and dripped; the rabble beset us on all sides and swelled as we went, but at last we came to the gaily decorated chapel, a very bower of branches and leaves and coloured paper. The Hindu officials were already there and lined one wall, our Christians the opposite one, the crowd pouring in after us took up every available inch in the middle—a difficult audience. Conspicuous on the left was Krishna Murti, the *Karnam*, on the right sat fat old Nursana the Christian goldsmith, who also was to speak.

The meeting began. The audience grew a little restive when Benjamin's exhortations were followed by Nursana's improvisations, but Jeanie's sweet, clear voice singing a lyric produced wrapt silence. Then it was my turn. How is one to address a congregation like that? Thoughts went to the wind, but an old illustration remained.

"I will tell you a story." The audience, ready to wriggle at the first sense of boredom, sank into contented quiet.

"About that heart of wisdom," I went on, "which you have already heard about, how important it is to get it, and how difficult. Would we not all like one? To possess it would be *Moksha* [1] indeed. This is known to the enemy of mankind who would destroy their souls and prevent them getting *moksha*. One day he called a council in hell and all evil spirits came together.

"'How shall we prevent men from turning their hearts unto wisdom and finding *moksha*?' the devil propounded his conundrum.

[1] Salvation, deliverance.

" 'Set up *toddy*[1] shops,' suggested a little demon. 'When men drink they lose all sense.' "

Some of the audience began to laugh. Others nodded sagely, "True words."

" 'Still there are many who will not drink,' said the chief devil. 'How shall we prevent them seeking wisdom?'

" 'Money! make them think of money! When men begin to want more money they soon think of nothing else,' suggested an experienced bad spirit."

At this moment I glanced at the *Karnam.* Hitherto he had worn rather a supercilious air, as if he had expected a Christian meeting to be just ranting against idol worship; now he looked thoughtful. A wonder flashed through my mind as to whether he was addicted to the not infrequent habit of *Karnams* of taking bribes, falsifying land records, etc. He leaned forward with interest.

" 'Yes, about money, that is a good plan,' said the devil. 'It will catch most men. Yet some will remain who do not care for money and still want to go after wisdom. How catch such?'

" A silence followed in hell. At last an evil spirit arose. ' "To-morrow," is what we will say to such. "Certainly they must seek wisdom and salvation," we will tell them. Only to-day they are busy; they must put it off till to-morrow. "To-morrow" is a good word for them!' he laughed. And all hell clapped in applause.

"Perhaps more men lose salvation through that last device of the devil than through any other." I finished. "Teach me to number my days. Will there be a to-morrow for everyone sitting here? Who can say? Let us apply our hearts to wisdom now."

Krishna Murti came forward with great cordiality when the meeting was over. "Our Telugu words come to you.

[1] The intoxicating liquor prepared from the juice of the date palm.

These are true words. I want to hear more. When will there be another meeting ?"

"To-morrow, to-morrow. It is New Year's Day and we shall have services. We shall be pleased to see you if you will come."

At last Jeanie and I got back to a belated supper. The old year died while the jackals howled over the plain.

The strong sun of "to-morrow," to-day now, leaped over the horizon. We were having our early cup of tea when a shocked messenger arrived with ill tidings.

"Krishna Murti, the *Karnam*, who spoke to you last night, is dead." We sat up stupefied. "Yes, heart disease," confirmed George Pillay later on. "It is a great shock to us all."

Later in the day we made our way to the house, which was still surrounded by a crowd. An elderly woman relative beckoned us to a side room off the verandah.

"What shall we all do now ? There is that girl, his third wife, she is expecting a baby; if it will only be a son! He has no son. And such an unlucky day for a death! We shall have to leave the house. No one can live in it. How much rent will they ask for another, knowing our necessity. And only last night he was so well! He was very happy over something. He had been to some meeting. He never talks much to us, but he talked last night when he had his rice, he seemed happy. 'I have been to a meeting,' he kept on saying. 'I heard such good words. Wisdom, wisdom!' It cannot have been the Union meeting. He generally comes back cross and angry from that."

"It was our meeting," we told her, "the Christians' meeting." She was utterly astonished. "The Christians' meeting ? What, then, made him so happy ?"

At the evening service I looked out of the chapel window. A glow against the darkening Eastern sky had attracted my attention. Smoke drifted. There, out on the *maidan*, Krishna

Murti's funeral pyre flamed. Yesterday he had sat here with us, making resolves about " to-morrow."

And through the open chapel doors drifted in the bazaar noises, the hum of people talking and planning the things they would do " to-morrow."

* * * * *

Daily life, unmoved, keeps on with its demands. In Balji Tippamma's house I have a special pet who has started going to school.

" And she came back the first day," said her mother laughingly, " and played a new game, all by herself."

" What was that ? " I asked.

" I saw her go into the barn, and shut the door after her. Wondering what she wanted, I looked through a crack. She knelt down and put her little hands together, so, and repeated, ' Our Father, our Father. Thy kingdom. Amen.' It is what the children learn to pray in your school, I think."

It is, indeed. And little Soni's act was just a child's game —nothing but a child's imitative instinct ? Yet I felt suddenly deeply moved, as if something great had happened.

" Our Father. Thy kingdom. Amen." The little Hindu girl's memory—or was it an awakening little soul ?—had unfailingly picked out from her first day at school the most important thing.

The household was in a stir to-day. Soni's eldest sister was about to go to her husband. They sent a man to fetch her yesterday, and this day she was to leave.

" But she goes differently from others," said Radha with shining eyes. " Instead of tomtoms and feasts Tippamma called me and we had prayer for her new home. She goes with the assurance of God's blessing and did not weep, as they always do; she is not afraid."

Indian child brides going away to strangers move me to much pity often. A few days before, in a shepherd's house, I found the father and mother sitting together in great sadness; and by them crouched their little daughter, aged about eleven, crying bitterly.

"They have come to fetch her away," they explained. "That young man is her husband, and the elder one his father. His wife has just died. There is no other female relative to cook for them. The little one must come, they say."

The poor child, to have to go to entire strangers, and cope with household tasks as best she can—to mature there alone, with no other woman near her, and immediately become a wife. To put on children burdens too heavy for them, to confront tender girls with experiences meant for adults, seemed too pitiful. It is the system that is cruel. The people in that room were all very sorry; none of them were hard or callous, but "we must follow the custom."

This case in the shepherd's house was not one of normal circumstances. Ordinarily a girl would mature at home, and only then go to her husband's house; generally not yet as a permanent arrangement either; a prolonged visit back to the parental roof is customary. Also in most cases there would be a mother-in-law to welcome the little bride and teach her; but in India, as in other countries, mothers-in-law have a reputation! Whether empty, or full of female "in-laws," the new home has a pretty severe discipline awaiting the child bride.

* * * * *

Not that Christians have *their* path all smooth! In the *Mala* quarters we found David the teacher and his wife who is near her confinement as depressed as any "depressed classes."

"How are we to manage? Our relatives are twenty-five miles from the railway; it would cost a month's salary for one person's journey," they lamented. "This is a new place for us; the *dhobi* will not wash for Christians; we manage ourselves at ordinary times, but now? Please, you must help us and make some arrangement."

Many and various are the calls upon a missionary. They awaited us still when at dark we got back to the little Rest-House. A man stood waiting on the verandah—the teacher of the girls' school. His string of petitions was comprehensive.

"Please let me have leave. To-night I must go. To save loss of two hundred rupees. And will you kindly increase my salary? I cannot manage, with my family."

"But you have only the baby one year old!"

"I am educating three brothers. This place is not convenient for me, will you please transfer me to Dharmapalli? And the other teacher. . . ." Here followed insinuations against his assistant in the school. Before he had been settled Hindu visitors arrived with New Year's offerings of flowers and fruit, according to the charming Indian custom. Sitting down to supper at last a message reached us, "The women are ready." That is the nightly prayer-meeting in Radha's house to which we hurried down, and found a well-filled room.

White-haired old Peddamini sat amongst them. At sight of us she broke into laudations: "Such mercy! Such condescension! Any trouble will they take; I had but to ask and she wrote a letter to the *dhora* for me, even to the Collector, all my affairs she set forth plainly in it. . . ."

"Yet after urging me so," I interrupted her pæans, "and telling me it was of the utmost necessity you never delivered my letter."

"How did you know I did not give it?" she said, in no wise abashed.

"I met the *dhora* and asked him if he had had the letter; he said, no."

"Oh, you talked to him about me! What love! So he looked after me beautifully! It is your help, your favour; you even spoke to him of me, what kindness! . . ."

One had to let it go at that. Inscrutable to us are some of the thoughts of India. But now, in that little room, the women sitting round, the Bible open before Radha, we all met on ground less likely to be misinterpreted.

And so home with our lanterns at 10.30, while Scorpio rode overhead; the problems of the day, as consciousness faded into sleep, merging into little Soni's prayer, "Our Father. Thy Kingdom. Amen."

CHAPTER III

THE hot weather is upon us. I am not wanting to swear, but with simple and sincere conviction I want to say, " The heat is infernal."

The grass has long ago been scorched: banyans and acacias are stark and bare; the earth burns you through your shoes; the stones and rocks are searing to the touch; the air is a hot mush; there is nothing fit to breathe, to stand on, sit on, lie on, let alone to eat! The land is a burning glare, the sun a relentless enemy; every event an irritation. I cannot be nice to the servants. " Oh, to be in England now that April's here! " April in South India unfits every temper for every strain—anyhow mine! But there is the prospect of the hills and coolness looming nearer too, so the powers of evil are not having it all their own way, even in April.

They seem to though, here, at present. Bad news brought me to Bukkuru, and I find the actual even worse than my fears. My dearly loved girls' school here has collapsed. The wave of *Swarajism* sweeping over the land has reached quiet, distant Bukkuru. A few wily spirits gave it access to simpler understandings, and now all are filled with it. It began during my furlough. On return I found the school empty; but we started it again. An old Brahmin here is the soul and mainstay of a new rival school. I am going to try a course of straightforward conciliatoriness with him.

* * * * *

Later. Hope is raising its head. When the Brahmin arrived I could feel that he was full of inward triumph, for nearly all our girls go to his school; outwardly he was suave and polite.

"See here, Mr. Sita Ramana," I began. "We desire the good of the town and of the children, both you and I, do we not? Now we Christians have had this school for a good many years; the parents were contented to send their children; there was peace. Now there is confusion and strife. Why should we oppose one another? Let us join forces. The town is not large enough for two schools. We have a good building, you have none. We will give ours. Expenses we will share equally; we shall have a Christian teacher, and you can nominate a Hindu one. I reserve of course the right to have Bible teaching in the school."

"I want to be co-manager," he replied.

"Well, why not? Why should we missionaries not associate ourselves with the people of this country whenever we can in some beneficent endeavour? We have practically no school and no children now. In a joint affair the Mission will have a voice in the management, it can appoint a Christian teacher, hold a Sunday School and have the entry to sixty houses. Would it not be worth while?" If only it comes off!

Mr. Sita Ramana went away to consult his school committee, and will let me know their decision.

It may help me to possess my soul in patience to go visiting with Radha. In a merchant's house we found a big group of women, amongst them a new-comer from another town, who listened earnestly.

"I can see," she said, "that your mind is stayed on God. You have learned it; your words are high. But we, how are we to learn it?"

I thought of the long cart drive here in the heat yesterday; how disturbed and anxious over the school news I felt all the time; and am I not possessed by anxiety at this moment? What are Sita Ramana's committee saying to my proposals? To stay one's mind on God is a hard lesson for us all.

A man came in who had travelled in " many countries," of India, that is; from Telugu he lapsed into Kanarese, and seemed pleased to receive an answer in that tongue. Languages became the topic. Many and varied are they in this world, but one only has the next. It took a little while to lead the audience to guess that, the great language of Love!

> " Some day or other I shall surely come
> Where true hearts wait for me,
> Then let me learn the language of that home
> While here on earth I be,
> Lest my poor lips for want of words be dumb
> In that high company."

gave me my inspiration.

No word had come from Sita Ramana on my return Saturday evening. Sunday morning came, and with it the duty of taking the service. It was hot! I had no freshness; the evening before a million mosquitoes made it impossible to sit by the lantern and read in preparation; also I was tired after the talks and visits in the town; so this morning, being ill-prepared, I could not grip the people. I felt it was my fault; there would have been resources, but I did not reach them.

Still no word from the Brahmin. At last I sent a request for an interview. He reported that his people would not agree to having Christian books or a Sunday School; the latter seemed a great dread of theirs; they evidently think it has a tremendous influence.

" Do you think you could call the Committee ? " I asked. " Let us talk it over together."

He went, and in a short time the chapel was filled to overflowing with all the important people of the town. I felt a little nervous at having to face this assembly alone. Collecting scraps of courage, I addressed the men in much the same way that I had addressed Sita Ramana in private, and made the same proposals.

A voluble speaker rose. Summed up his speech was this: "You have taught our children for some years. Here is the harvest; we see now that girls ought to be educated, and can do it ourselves."

"I rejoice in that," I replied. "Can we not still go on together? You say you are grown up, but I do not see in this country that when children grow up they cut themselves adrift from their parents."

More and more speeches. They were against anything Christian or Western; Christian books, Bible classes, anything definite. We talked for hours. They came round to some extent, though they insisted on Bible classes being excluded from the regular time-table, and attendance at Sunday School being entirely optional. (It always has been.) But a Christian teacher is to be allowed. I drew up the list of conditions into an agreement which both sides are to sign. To-morrow I meet the Inspectress to lay this novel arrangement before her; it is fortunate that she happens to be in this neighbourhood.

* * * * *

Alas! all my hopes for the school are dashed. The carefully drawn-up conditions were re-discussed all the evening by the people in their temple. Late at night the Catechist came and told me the result was: we will not amalgamate.

It was a great blow. They had seemed practically won over. Perhaps they shrank from pledging themselves in a written bond. It means—I choke as I write it—the closing of our loved girls' school here. If I still tried to keep it on Sita Ramana would, as soon as my back was turned, begin his previous tactics of carrying off bodily the few girls that still loyally come to our school. I cannot leave instructions with the teacher or conductress to have a hand-to-hand scuffle over a pupil with the rival party! Instead of laying before the Inspectress a new scheme of amalgamation, I shall simply have to inform her of the closing of the Mission school.

* * * * *

It was a melancholy interview, yet it proved not wholly cheerless. It took place at Patacheruvu, two miles from here. The Inspectress told me what had just happened in that place. The Hindus had started a girls' school, a most praiseworthy affair, financing it themselves till they could get Government recognition. This they at length obtained. With the financial aid the Department used its prerogative of appointing teachers. The people had no thought other than that a Hindu teacher would be sent. But the unexpected happened. The Inspectress appointed a Christian headmistress. The town heard it with consternation. A Christian woman, of low caste of course, was to instruct the high caste girls of the town? The townspeople would not accept the blow. Brahmins and others petitioned against it in writing; a deputation awaited the Inspectress at the station to voice verbally and plainly their disapproval of the Christian's appointment.

The Assistant Inspectress, herself an Indian Christian, though dismayed at this opposition, remained firm.

"I told them I had no other trained teacher for the post. Then whom do you think they suggested? A *Bogum* [1] girl, not trained, whom we had tried as a teacher, but had to get rid of for bad conduct. This candidate they pressed upon me, saying she wished to be away from her former surroundings where she could not be good; and that by giving her a post in a new place we should help her to a better life."

Help her, yes; though being a *Bogum* and already having entered that life, reclamation by mere change of scene is doubtful.

[1] Dancing girl. Practically synonymous with professional prostitute.

Meanwhile what about the children? There seems to be little comprehension of such psychological subtleties as unconscious influence. "She will only teach reading." There would not emanate from such a one a lowering of the moral standards? a subtle minimizing of the value of purity, straightness, and sterling character? Often India seems blind to that; for one meets it again and again. How frequent is the petition to retain an unworthy person: "He is a poor man, he has a large family, you must keep him in his post!" The part, immediately in front of one's eyes, counts in Indian eyes; the whole—shadowy in the background—is overlooked. Not that in this case the real, or, anyhow, chief care was for the saving of the *Bogum* girl. The heart of the matter was opposition to a Christian, presumably low caste, woman.

It was not an easy position for the young Inspectress herself, newly appointed to this post; she has her way to make in this district; reports may be sent to her superior officer with who knows what misconstructions! But this Christian girl, for the first time away from her family, finding solitary touring among villages full of hardship, and the responsibilities of her post oppressive, remained firm in her refusal of a teacher of doubtful morality.

It was in a mango garden we had our interview, for the town offered no chance of private talk; the trees were still too young for shade, but the watchman's little hut sheltered us against the pitiless sun; the hot air quivered round us as we discussed many problems.

"There are far too few women teachers; why don't you educate more Christian girls and train them to be teachers? Every year now we are opening more girls' schools and shall need more women teachers," the Assistant Inspectress urged.

Through the white glare of the bare country beyond the garden a vision rose on me: crowded towns, busy little townlets, sunbaked villages, and girls' schools everywhere;

and in each, Christian women teachers: the educating, the moulding of impressionable girls throughout South India, in Christian hands. Did not this fact of their desiring a woman of evil life as instructress for their children show how badly Christian standards were needed? Public opinion needed altering. And how could this better be done than by impressing Christian ideals upon the young? And where get at them better than in schools?

And that plaint of the woman yesterday, "How are we to learn to set our minds on God?" can they learn it in one afternoon's talk? The memory of little Soni in the barn, playing at prayer—or was it, rather, the beginning of setting her mind on God?—flashed through my mind. We must teach the children before life hardens them; we must have more boarding homes for Christian village girls; we must have our own training institutions for teachers—fair and fairer the outlook widened.

With a shock I came back to earth. Boarding homes, training schools—where is the staff, where the finance?

Instead, we have lost the school we had in Bukkuru. No more will little Sonis learn to go straight to the heart of things.

Yards have gone in Bukkuru. But here in Patacheruvu one little inch is gained through the appointment of a Christian mistress.[1]

Lost yards, however, bulk largely; gained inches are microscopic. Jogging back to Bukkuru in the furnace of

[1] *Note in later years.* The Christian headmistress came and worked in the school many years. When she died all the town went to her funeral, Brahmins, merchants, officials, high caste people; all had been so impressed by her work and her goodness that they were eager to do her this last honour. Her husband had been appointed in one of the boys' schools where he rose to the position of headmaster. The townspeople came to him and said, "We will pay the expenses of a second marriage for you; get an educated Christian girl that she may teach our children; we want such an one as your late wife." His second wife occupies that post now.

the midday heat the enemy of depression beset me hard. There is not a single thing just now that is not discouraging. The catechist here, for some reason, has sent in his resignation. The school has gone; the atmosphere in the town is hostile; the workers are dispirited. Radha for some days had been saying she could not talk to parents any more about sending their children to school; she met too much abuse. "You need not try again," I told her yesterday, "the school is closed." Then she was heart-broken. After my return from Patacheruvu there she stood, saying she had been to houses but could not talk to people; there was too big a lump in her throat; she had better stay at home.

"To sit and weep? That is, of course, what God wants us to do now. Or perhaps there is no God at all, seeing things have all gone wrong. Or if He is there, He has no doubt forsaken us; forsaken our work in Bukkuru anyhow," I chaffed her, feeling myself rather as she did.

"They say in the town that now all the Christians will be driven out," lamented poor Radha.

"Well, let us go to the houses and tell them they will not."

"Which houses?" said Radha, still in the Slough of Despond.

"We will find some," I responded, climbing resolutely out myself.

Was it mere human contrariness? Or some undeserved but much needed wave of help from unseen encouragers? Without reason or sense, cheerfulness flooded my consciousness. More than that, a sense of triumph. Whence came it? In the depth, in the dark, with no visible sign of success anywhere; yet a sense of triumph.

We went to the town, towards the house of an old schoolgirl.

Before reaching it a woman stepped in front of us and salaamed courteously.

" I am sent to ask you to come to our school."

" Your school? Which is that? I do not know of any other girls' school in this town."

" It is the Mohammedan girls' school."

Full of astonishment we followed her. She led us through various streets to a private house. In a room off the courtyard a smiling Mohammedan woman greeted us, and a dozen or so little girls salaamed respectfully.

We learned that this little school had been established privately for about two months; that more girls were anxious to come; that this teacher was asking the Mission to take over the school.

I listened dumbfounded. Was this God's way out? It is a way that had never occurred to me. The more I thought the more it seemed like a miracle. " We will kill the Christian school, we will drive Christianity out of Bukkuru," is the present resolve of Brahmins, I understand. But over a Mohammedan school they will have no control. We have lost the old; but here was a little new school, it would seem, all quietly prepared of God.

But mixed with wonder and gratitude, doubts and difficulties raised gorgon heads.

" Mohammedans speak Hindustani. I do not know that language. This Mohammedan teacher happens to know Telugu, but Hindustani would be the medium of instruction. What time is there to learn it? And what a labour! Yet how could I control the work of the school not knowing the written characters and unable to question the scholars? And what about this woman? I do not even know whether she is respectable! "

That, however, by various inquiries, was soon ascertained. She is married and her old father who lives in the house is one of the most respected Mohammedans here.

Now one comes to think of it, here beginneth a new education for our Christians. Hitherto, passing Mohammedan houses, Radha had said, " These are not our people," though many of them understand Telugu quite well; now, cheered by the prospect of another Mission girls' school in the town, her usual enthusiasm flamed up. " I am going to visit all these new houses," she burst forth. The fresh interest I prayed for had come, and come this very same day!

The Telugu Christian woman teacher in our former school was tackled. " Will you teach in the new school? "

" I cannot. I do not know the language, I do not know these people."

" Never mind, learn it. At first teach only sewing, and meanwhile every day you can pick up a letter or two of the alphabet. When you know five or six you could teach some infants who know none. Every day the Mohammedan teacher will teach you ordinary words. See, I will learn it too."

Later. It has actually been arranged, I have taken over the school; to-day we had our first sewing lesson. A number of Mohammedan women crowded in to have a good look. " Are you going to teach our children? It is well. You are father and mother to them now."

Giriappa, the Christian teacher's husband, came up with a shining face. " They have been saying, 'We have killed your school; we will kill the whole mission.' We did not know how to hold up our heads, but this is the help of God, we have a school here still."

" A very present help in trouble."

But I cannot help mourning over our lost Hindu girls' school, I loved it much.

There is a time to mourn, doubtless; but in the Mission field it has to be curtailed; I shall have to spend my holidays getting hold of Hindustani; I hope I can find some sort of a *munshi* [1] while on the hills!

[1] Teacher.

CHAPTER IV

PARALLEL with the main bazaar street of Andapur containing nothing but shops runs a street inhabited almost exclusively by Brahmins. Thoughtfully I walked through it one evening. How are we to set about winning an entrance here? Dorcas goes mostly to middle-class homes. Surely these others ought not to be entirely neglected. The problem must be attacked.

I am making the discovery that its climate makes India a country of wonderful accessibility. There are no shut doors and forbidding house-fronts as in England; doors stand open all day long; on friendly *pials* [1] people sit and chat and watch the goings on in the street. It is not difficult when passing to stand still and ask the women on the *pial* a casual question. After the first time of asking one may next time nod to them as acquaintances; after that one progresses to asking leave to sit on the *pial* too. Reception then varies: sometimes they are just full of curiosity or, sometimes shyness; sometimes they appear very willing to be friendly; but almost always I am conscious of a sense of superiority in the air. Are they not Brahmins? And who am I? No one of any standing evidently, or should I be walking there alone with no one at all, not even one *peon* [2] behind me?

Anyhow there, to-day, I sat on the *pial* with two Brahmin women with whom I had become acquainted in this slender fashion. Presently an older widow came and sat down by us.

"Amma," [3] I turned to her searching for an opening, "you are farther on in the way of life than I am; is not

[1] Small mud or stone platforms along a house-front, or round a tree.

[2] Servant, messenger.

[3] Mother, woman, mistress, etc. The ordinary word for addressing any Telugu woman.

our life given us to learn wisdom? If, then, I ask you to tell me a word of wisdom, it is right, is it not? What word will you tell me?"

"No one teaches us words of wisdom," she replied.

"Is it true then?" I said. "I heard in my country that many are left without words of wisdom. May I tell you some they teach where I come from?"

A beginning was made. Nearly an hour slipped by. A number of widows had drifted to the *pial.* A late comer, again a Brahmin, said, "Come to our house." When we had arrived there she collected still others and commanded, "Now tell them all that again."

But instead, I ventured to come out with a proposal that had been maturing in my mind. "I should so like to have a meeting of ladies here in the town," I submitted. "I hear you used to have one in one another's houses; but it only lasted a few weeks; could we not start it again? Will you help me?"

"*You* ask *our* help?" they said in astonishment.

"Please, if you will," I went on, "and may I tell you something else? Two days ago I sat much troubled in my bungalow because I was wanting to get to know you all, and I asked God to show me a way. You all believe in prayer, do you not? Now here to-day I have been led to your house and you are willing to help; is it not God's kindness?"

"Yes, yes, we will help you and tell the others. Come again on Friday, we will be ready."

* * * * *

This is Friday evening—and what a day!

When I sped to town in the early afternoon to my Brahmin friends I looked forward to finding not only them but the others they promised to collect.

But no one sat on the *pial.* A knock at the door elicited

at first no response. At last one or two women came out looking utterly depressed.

A chill of disappointment passed through me. Had they wholly changed? But it could not be merely that; trouble was in the air.

"Amma, what is the matter?" I inquired.

"The child is very ill."

"I am so sorry, may I come in?"

Dubious looks. "We will see."

Some debating went on inside, while I waited in the street. Then they invited me in, and I stepped into a room full of sorrow.

Someone told me the family history. Three little sons had gone, always at that age of three or four, of fever and convulsions; and here was the fourth and last, three years old, in the grip of the same dreaded symptoms.

The father, a man of English education, had hurriedly come from his office and sat by his little son, the mother lay on the other side beside him, four widowed aunts sat along the wall.

I asked questions, was allowed to feel the pulse; begged them to prepare hot water for a bath; pressed them to call in the doctor.

"We have; but there is an inspection at the hospital, the Chief Medical Officer from Madras is here, so the doctor has not come."

"I will go and get him."

Away on the cycle, to the doctor's house first, in case he was there. No, he was out; seeing me standing there the neighbours beckoned me in to pour out their tale of woe. This woman has had twelve children; six have lived. Since the birth of the last one she is so weak she cannot move at all. Her eldest daughter is now helping her; her husband has gone off to Burmah; no word of him has come for two years. "Oh, our trouble, our trouble," they said, "no one has such trouble as we."

Perhaps; but the other people's trouble was more immediately urgent; I could not stay long to sympathize. Reaching the hospital I found the official inspection going on and every one distracted and busy; but I got speech with the Assistant Surgeon who promised to go to Bima Rao's house as soon as possible. Walking by the women's ward I noticed a patient sitting alone on her cot, tears dribbling down her cheeks, looking so forlorn that I could not pass her.

"What is it, *amma*?"

"They have cut off my leg," she wailed.

Poor soul, comfort is at present difficult. "They will give you a nice new one of wood and then you will have no pain and be able to walk again," I tried to cheer her. But that prospect seems not very believable just now.

Meeting so many dismal things in this one hour caused Yeats's lines to drift into my mind.

> "Come away, oh human child,
>
> . . . . .
>
> With a fairy hand in hand,
> For the world is full of weeping,
> More than you can understand."

But there was no fairyland in this Indian town. Dusk was falling; on the way home I got mixed up with a herd of goats; they were skittish and I in a great hurry; a spill ensued; never mind, no bones broken—a bottle of Brand's essence must be fetched, and so back to my Brahmins' house.

Weeping and wailing greeted me. Was I too late? No, only another fit; but it passed soon. It was dark inside; the lamp was lit; its light so tiny that it seemed to increase the gloom of that sad interior: the poor, sorrow-stricken father sitting there dumb; the weeping mother curling herself like a snake, so thin and lissom was she, round the child;

the widows in their red *saris* sitting near, some crying, some mute in stony despair; the hope of all these people lying in their midst, apparently dying. The doctor had not yet called.

"May I give my medicine?" I ventured.

Oh yes, anything, anything now; no caste or any other prejudices counted at such a moment, only save him.

It seemed to me the child was sinking from sheer weakness; I opened the Brand's essence and was allowed to administer it; and they strict Brahmins! I talked as cheerily as I could; for such an atmosphere of utter hopelessness could be good for no patient. With the courage of lay ignorance I assured them the pulse was now a little stronger; indeed, I was praying, willing, concentrating myself on increase of vitality.

All night I think I dreamed about the Brahmin child; first thing in the morning I cycled round to inquire. Thank God, he was better. The Assistant Surgeon had come at night; they showed him my "medicine," the Brand's essence, which he praised and told them to go on giving. Very thankfully I went out.

In the street I met a *vakil* [1] I know, who professes advanced views; I seized the chance to tackle him about the possibility of a ladies' meeting.

"That is a very good idea," he said, "I will help you all I can and send messages to every one."

I thanked him most gratefully, and asked him to define time and place. We fixed Wednesday.

As I was passing the door of Mr. Rama Krishna Rao whose wife I knew, I thought I would look in and invite them myself. There I had a shock. On former visits I had met a sister, Tangamma, a young widow; as I did not see her in the room I inquired after her. Their faces fell; no one answered.

The *Gavali* [2] woman bringing milk had just come in;

[1] Lawyer. [2] Name of a caste of cowherds.

standing by the door she heard my question; when no one answered she broke the silence.

"She slipped and fell into the well, and died," I was informed.

"Oh, poor Tangamma!" I said in distress. "How could it happen? Which well?"

"The one in the garden," volunteered the milk woman. "It was early in the morning."

But here in the courtyard was their ordinary drawing-well. In the morning water for the household would be drawn here. A horrible doubt beset me. Why should Tangamma go alone so very early to the well in the garden? Did she "slip and fall in"?

"She had no joy in life," someone said, as if reading my grave suspicions.

They evidently shared them, then. Poor Tangamma, still quite young, had been unable to face the desolate prospect of long years, leading nowhere, bringing no change, holding no possible joy.

There are thousands of them, these girl widows; millions I believe, taking in all India; but I could not think of figures just then—just this one filled my horizon. Here she had been in the very town where I lived, slowly breaking her heart, slowly sinking into irremediable despair. There had been no word for her of hope; no hand to hold her back from the crime against herself. If only there were women of enlightenment and hearts of love who had time to stay here, making friends among these high caste people! If Tangamma could have learned to look upon such a one as a friend might it have made a difference to her?

* * * * *

To-day is Tuesday, and I have something to report. In the morning I resolved to go round and remind the women about to-morrow's meeting. I went first to my little patient's house, where this week has advanced me by leaps and bounds in intimacy. He is fast recovering; when they speak of him to me it is as " your son."

But about the meeting they were dubious. " To-morrow is not a lucky day; to-day would be better."

" Very well; I will go and tell the others."

" Please invite Adi Murti Rao's family too," they suggested.

" But I have never called there yet; how can I go in the morning when the men are at home and the women busy ? "

" Oh yes, go, never mind," they repeated.

My forecasts, however, proved true. The door was closed. I stood in the blazing sunshine and knocked. After a long time a woman came. " What is it ? " she said.

" May I come in ? " I asked, longing to get out of the heat.

" The men have bathed, we have bathed," i.e. no contact with a defiling outsider can be risked now.

I explained through the half-open door.

" We may come," was the half-hearted reply.

I went on to other houses.

" We may come."

" We cannot come to-day."

" If so and so comes, we will come too."

In one house only was there the heartening reply, " We will come whether anyone else comes or not." That was the Sub-Inspector's (of schools) house; he seemed delighted that his wife was invited.

It was interesting being in their houses in the morning. The men were about, half-dressed, sometimes chatting with friends in the verandah; beggars came chanting and received doles; in one house they were cooking, and did not seem to care if I cast a defiling glance on it or not; that was in " my son's " house. In one house the reply to the invitation was the usual, " We must ask the men "—then a pause.

"Yes, let us ask them," I prodded.

"He is at prayer."

I composed myself to wait. Minutes passed, more minutes, many minutes. "Long prayers it seems in the world they say,"[1] I thought, sitting there like another forsaken merman. Perhaps forlornness, or possibly impatience, were written too plainly on me. "He will come directly," someone who had gone to see informed me. How, I wondered, with my Western notion of prayer, could they tell when a man would finish praying? It was the house of the Public Prosecutor; he came at last and said courteously "I am sorry you had to wait, I was at my prayers." Mentally I tried to put the speech into the mouth of an English lawyer, and found it would not go in.

The religiousness of India! At once our great hope and our despair; for too often it is but religious ceremonialism, easily performed, easily spoken of, making talk on religious subjects natural, but blocking the way to the understanding of true religion as much as it did in the days of Jesus Christ. Yet it must indicate a deeper feeling somewhere.

At two o'clock I sent Suleiman to call my guests. I did not know whether any would come besides the Sub-Inspector's wife, but three cartloads drew up, eighteen women and many children; all Brahmins, and every one a new friend made within the week.

"We had to come," they said, "seeing all the trouble you took this morning."

They were all eagerness to look over the bungalow. "How clean it is," they remarked, "and what a lot of room for one person." It was good to see that gorgeously robed crowd moving about the rooms as if they were quite at home. Finally we were all settled in the study, and the harmonium came into action. Some kind guardian angel must have improved my voice for the occasion, or lent them

[1] M. Arnold: *The Forsaken Merman*.

kind ears; they seemed impressed by the sweetness and solemnity of "Lead, kindly Light."

I explained the hymn a little. "Is it not a prayer for us all?"

"Oh yes, a beautiful prayer," they readily agreed.

"She does not even say the name," I heard one woman say to another in an admiring voice. It had not been at all intentional on my part; I had taken the hymn as it was; but she evidently thought my omission of Christ's name premeditated courtesy towards them and consequently thought of Him herself.

Several of the guests were prevailed upon to sing, mostly young girls. Christmas cards, made into needle-cases, and Telugu magazines were then brought forth for the women and small dolls for the little girls, these last gifts evidently causing some envy in the hearts of their elders.

"We must go now, you have given us great pleasure," said the polite guests when I warmly thanked them for coming. "Could we have another meeting?" I asked, "perhaps in the school?"

"Many more will come there," they responded.

"Which day next week?" I pressed them.

"We will send you word."

After they left I paid a flying visit to the hospital to try and comfort the poor desolate patient of yesterday. The sun was setting yellow and stormy, the northern sky was alive with sheet lightning. On return I sat in the darkening compound and watched that living sky. Feeling in need of food for mind and soul as well I took a volume of J. B. Brierley and by lantern light started reading, only to be interrupted immediately by the information that the calf had drunk all the milk. *That* cowman!

Undeterred, I continued and came on helpful things. "Jesus found the Messianic idea there. He did not say 'Away with it,' though it was material, earthly, limited.

He linked Himself to it, refined it, enlarged it, spiritualized it, till it became the idea of a World Redeemer."

Is it not even so here? Here also we come not to destroy, but to fulfil. We, too, have to link ourselves to the aspirations we find in India. That is so much more lovely a work than to overthrow them. I go through the bazaar now and look at it with different eyes. These hundreds of people, each, deep down, with their longings for God, feeble, flickering, choked perhaps often, yet real. To fulfil them! To present to them that incomparable Figure who alone can!

To-day I met echoes of yesterday. One Brahmin woman from whom I had previously met so cool a reception that I had not ventured to ask her to the bungalow, now accosted me.

"I hear that they all came to see you yesterday; why did you not call us?" she reproached me. I apologized profusely.

"We would all have come! And you gave them dolls and needle-cases and books of good words. I want a doll and a book of good words."

"Will you come next week here to the school when other ladies will come?"

Certainly she would. But such promises are not to be counted on too firmly; dolls cannot be forthcoming every time either. Was I raising quite wrong expectations when simply an advance in friendliness was intended? How to show these people in simple ways which cannot be misinterpreted that one cares for them? This horrible caste, I anathematized, why cannot one ask them to meals and go to meals with them and be just ordinarily sociable; at home every friendly function always includes (not to say culminates in) sharing food and drink. What is a missionary in India to do instead of this?

I was passing the door of one of our Brahmin pupils. Three widows live there; Kallamma's mother and aunt and her elder sister, the latter alas! a childless girl widow, not yet shaved, but as they are very strict she soon will be. I paused to speak to them.

"Our brother is so ill," said the two older women sadly, "come in and see him."

I found he had pneumonia. The doctor had been called, and fomentations and turpentine were in use. The one thing needed was nourishment. Invalid food preparation is a thing that should be taught in all schools! In some Indian homes they know how to make it, but in many more they do not, and there is a strange prejudice against milk.

Diffidently I offered "medicine," thinking of Brand's essence again. "May I get it?"

"Yes, we will take it if it agrees with the other medicine."

The serviceable cycle soon had me home and back again; they accepted the offering and actually fed him in front of me. Again, orthodox Brahmins!

They were so troubled—their one man! I sat there with them in the dusk and felt the pitifulness of their lot. Being widows, throughout this long hot day they had not touched a morsel of food as it was a fast day; nor—and this seems to me torment unbearable—a drop of water. They had not eaten since yesterday midday and will not till to-morrow midday, though water is allowed to-morrow morning.

I remembered my Radha telling me about her experiences in the past. For years she observed all the fast days of the Brahmin widows; she described how cracked and swollen the throat becomes in the hot weather, so that when one drinks the next day one can hardly swallow, though all night one has not slept for thirst. And to this torture the young girl sitting there in front of me would soon be condemned; as soon as shaving has taken place all the rigour of the fasting and other laws comes into operation. Poor Tangamma! Was it perhaps unbearable thirst that caused her to make an end? What right has any human being to impose such things on another?

Naturally the sufferers are women. True, there are the *sanyasis* with their mortifications of the body; but what a world of difference there is between choosing a life of austerities of your own free will, and being compelled! This fast day is compulsory for Brahmin widows and comes twice a month. As I watched these two older women sitting there, their wan, tired figures and patient, care-worn faces and reflected that in their foodless state and exhausted by anxiety they had all the nursing to do, the piteous hardness of their life went to my very heart. How steep is their way of holiness!

Dinner to-night will stick in my throat. Since coming back from the stifling town I have drunk a tumbler of lime juice and water; I felt like a glutton.

All the time I am thinking anxiously about the sick brother of these poor women. I fervently hope he will get better; and I also hope he will never know what he has taken; they told me he was very pious!

A week later. He has been getting on not unsatisfactorily I think; but fever continues high. I went to the town this morning—and what a morning! Going eastwards I met the breeze; the rocky hills shone gloriously in the sun, the waves of the tank,[1] which is still well filled, rippled with morning merriment; in the great stretches of rice fields the joy of the harvest ran riot. Everywhere picturesque groups were dotted about, dense crowds of coolies round some headman, the crowds broke up and single figures dived into the sheen of yellow green. A sense of gladness pervaded the landscape; it laughed in the breeze; it rippled in the water; it shone from the fields and the cheerful, chattering workers as they stooped into the mass of stalks; a morning of such exhilaration as to make even a missionary compose poetry! anyhow a hymn (I apologize to the hymn for the antithesis), but unfortunately I can do neither

[1] Artificial lake.

In the house of my pneumonia patient there was no morning glory, rather midnight gloom. He looked much worse; the pain was less but the weakness appalling; I fear he is starving. They have called in a native doctor; I dare not start on another pot of Brand's. It was different when they had the Assistant Surgeon; for he and I understood each other about that; but if a native doctor found out what Brand's was and told the patient he might consider his salvation lost, and all Brahmin houses would be closed to me.

The sick man moved his hand towards me in some appeal; I bent to catch his difficult whisper: "Ground hard, get cot from hospital," was the petition. He may have bed sores, poor man; but the hospital would not lend their cots to private houses. "There is the old camp cot," I remembered luckily. "Yes, you shall have one, I will send it directly," I assured him. By this time I hope he is established upon it, for I sent it at once on my return. Perhaps he will think there is white magic in it!

* * * * *

The day is past and over—the day of the ladies' gathering in the school—and now, in the evening I say with a full heart, "All thanks, O Lord, to Thee!"

First I looked in at my patient. There sat my orthodox Brahmin on the old cot—sat up! though much propped, of course. When he saw me he made a *namaskaram* [1] and breathed: "Sleep came." His family told me that through my great and infinite merit in sending the cot he had been able to sleep soundly, the first night after many sleepless ones, and felt much stronger this morning.

How easy it is to gain merit. Merely an order to a servant and it was finished; they think no end of it. Of the real efforts, the things that cost, they think nothing at all.

[1] Salutation of respect.

I went into the school, hoping for a crowd. One woman sat there. "Two others came and went away again; they will come back," she cheered me kindly. Gradually three or four more arrived; children, filled with curiosity, pressed in from the street; the Brahmin ladies looked askance at them and drew back their *saris*. My heart sank a little. The harmonium had been brought down; its aid was now brought into play; a few schoolgirls acted as choir; more women drifted in, but there was so much coming and going that the quiet meeting I had planned seemed impossible. When about twenty women were present the young rabble from the street was firmly expelled and the door closed. Then for a moment I feasted my eyes on the realization of a dream: here in our school, a little gathering of Brahmin women from the town. Might I read to them? I asked, and saw doubt in some faces.

"From a book of prayers written some hundreds of years before the time of Christ," I went on and noticed relief. Evidently they feel shy of anything like frontal attacks! The 139th Psalm was read and talked about very simply. At the end I asked them should we meet again? Was it not good to talk and think together sometimes about spiritual things, since we all needed them? Most of them agreed warmly. "The men may stop us from coming," some said doubtfully. Others more encouragingly, "More will come."

Anyhow a beginning has been made. When I look at my despair about work in this town last week and reflect that it is only nine days since Andapur has been tackled with determination, and that within that time we have had a reception in the bungalow and a gathering in the school, it seems promising, does it not? Now it needs to be followed up; but I am due in camp—for the thousandth time I sigh for a colleague!

CHAPTER V

THE carts moved slowly across country; for five days the sun had been shining after a spell of rain; the track must be dry now, I thought, and Bhagyamma and I were *en route* for Taramulla. But the black clay soil retains the moisture which neither drains away nor evaporates; its treachery kept the usual tedium of the journey easily at bay. An innocent-looking puddle may mean that a wheel will go in suddenly a foot deep; the balance of the two-wheeled cart becomes precarious to an alarming degree. "Let us get out!" shrieked Bhagyamma when a wheel had thus sunk in and threatened to go on descending. "Yes, this time we are certainly going to die," I said in response to her spirit, if not her words.

"You are laughing, I believe," said Bhagyamma suspiciously. "Always you laugh when there is trouble."

The driver had got off, coaxing his animals to unheard-of efforts.

"Our Missiamma is pleased at the bad road," Bhagyamma called to him vindictively; "she is laughing."

Incurable optimists, I admit, are the most irritating of people to those otherwise gifted; I appreciated her need of blackening my character to somebody.

"She is laughing, is she?" grinned the cart man unsympathetically when he had heaved us out of danger again. Hard is the lot of pessimists.

Though some of our escapes were truly narrow, the satisfaction of an upset or a hopeless stick-fast was not granted by a callous fate. We arrived safely in the little tamarind grove under the hill, though our feet, instead of being the beautiful ones of real heralds of good tidings, were mud-caked atrocities. Mine made me feel a spectacle to all men; to the angels doubtless also, but they considerately refrained from making me feel worse by keeping out of sight. Which was more than the world of Taramulla did. Their unstinted stares were our embarrassing portion; fortunately the pitching of the tent offered a fresh scent, but my idea of writing meanwhile brought them back in full cry. "She writes without ink, yet ink is there," word passed round among a crowd who had never heard of fountain pens. Two girls who are old acquaintances pressed through and boldly inquired the price of this magic. One was the widowed daughter of the postmaster here, and the sight of her brought back a host of problems: how to persuade her father to let her go and study in Andapur; how to house her safely when she gets there; the young lives wasted and wasting in villages everywhere need an army of us to go after them and find them.

Nor is it only girls. In this village there are some families of the old royal caste, *Raju* people whose women are kept secluded. In this respect they differ from the rest of the Hindu community in South India whose women may all go out.[1] From their former high estate the *Rajus* have sunk to that of simple and often poor landowners. When I visited Taramulla the first time they sent a request for a call.

A pale and tired-looking woman met me in the first house. "Have you been ill, *amma*?" I asked.

"A month ago my baby was born," she replied listlessly. Others volunteered the further information that the little son had not lived, and that the same sad fate had befallen the first son. "She has a bad *karma*," [2] was their explanation of these facts.

[1] It is in the North that women of better classes are kept *gosha* in zenanas, as also all Mohammedan women throughout India.

[2] Originally *activity*, but denoting, according to Hindu philosophy, the fate self-created by sin contained in activity.

Nanchara herself acquiesced in the dictum of hopelessness. "Yes, my *karma* is bad," she repeated.

Is it thus any of us are meant to live? One's soul revolted against this tyranny of despair and offered battle.

"Nanchâramma, listen. You have seen a blind person? Once there was a man born blind, very poor; though he had parents they could not support him; he sat by the wayside, begging. He had not even a memory of what human faces looked like, or the sky, or flowers. You would call it a bad *karma*? He, too, had no son. For who would marry a blind beggar?

"A great Teacher passed that way one day with His disciples.

"'What a bad *karma* is this beggar's,' said one disciple, 'to be blind.' 'He was born blind, so perhaps it is his parents,' said another. They began to discuss whose sin it was. But what did the Teacher Himself say?

"'*Neither has this man sinned, nor his parents; but that the works of God should be made manifest in him.*' He healed the blind eyes. Neither is it God's intention that anyone should sit in hopeless darkness now. He sent this Teacher and Saviour Who is called 'The Light of the World.' . . ."

An hour had slipped by unawares. Impatient messages came from the second *Raju* house. Here several families were living together, a household with over twenty women of all ages. "We hear you say good words, talk to us also," they urged.

A white-haired grandmother sat among them whose face was one "acquainted with grief." A little grandson surviving all her own children had been her great joy in life. When he fell ill he was taken in a cart to Ramidi dispensary as a last resort. In torment of anxiety she awaited the return. But it was only the poor lifeless body they brought home at dusk. The broken-hearted grandmother that night took a poisonous root to end her intolerable anguish. The others suspected and forced an emetic on her. Her sorrow-filled eyes turned towards me. "Have you any comfort?" they seemed to say.

"*Who has brought life and immortality to light.*" Those enemies He fought, disease, despair, grief, hopelessness, here confront us also at every turn, and in His name one may advance upon them; they are not meant to hold human lives in bondage. But it is a long and slow conquest. How much reached the old woman's heart in her stony despair I do not know. "Don't Christians die?" she asked wonderingly.

* * * * *

Evening. To-day thirteen or fourteen women awaited us in the big *Raju* house; one of them would scarcely allow time for ordinary greeting. "Don't ask us how we are," she said impatiently. "Tell, begin to tell; don't lose time."

"*You* ask that?" I said with a smile. "Last time you did not want to listen."

"No," she admitted. "I used to feel angry with God and against your religion. But it is different now."

Another woman had joined the household, a relative who had lost both husband and brother in one night from plague; she leaned forward and devoured what was being said.

"Still tell something; say more, don't go yet," was thrust at me whenever I rose to depart. It is difficult to gauge what to these secluded women in villages off the beaten track such visits from outside must mean. Nursamma, the head *Raju's* wife, pulled me aside afterwards.

"I have a request," she whispered. "I want you to have the care of my son. Please find a way. His father"—her whisper sank lower still—"is not a good man. My boy goes into the village street, I cannot follow him. I don't know what he sees and learns outside. Will you teach him? Deep down I feel your religion is the true one; ours has no help."

God help the anxious mother-heart. How are we to make the way she craves? A school might do it.

To-day in Nanchâramma's house I heard an astonishing story from her. "Last time you were here a girl from a neighbour's house came in and listened. You did not see her; she sat behind you by the door. When you had gone she asked, 'Who is that lady?' We told her the Mission lady from Andapur. She said, 'Then I will go to Andapur. These are the words I want, the words I have been waiting for all my life. I want no rice, no water even, if I can hear these words.'"

"Where is she now?" I broke in. "Why did she not come? What is her name? Was she married?"

"She was not married, though already eighteen. She was very unusual. Her family was greatly impressed by her piety. When she said 'Not yet, not yet,' about marriage, they listened to her. She was coming to you and went to tell her married sister. In that village cholera broke out; she nursed her sister through it, then fell ill herself. She died there. News came here that it was a very beautiful death. She called the elders of the village, and said, 'I know I am this day going to God, I am not afraid. Remember God, all of you.' And so she died."

Into my thoughts of regret at having missed an earnest and aspiring soul broke the present: "Talk to us now you are here," pressed the women.

The afternoon was far advanced when we left; I felt I had no more in me and was making for the tent; but in the lane a farmer's family sent a message. "The men are not here now, come and talk to us by ourselves." Half a dozen women sat expectant, others pressed in; among them a woman carrying two babes. "Twins?" Bhagyamma inquired.

"No, only this one is mine; that one's mother is dead, there is no one to look after it; I thought perhaps God will give me milk enough for two."

"He will not fail to bless you," I said with unstinted

admiration. Will not this ignorant village woman hear one day the words "Inasmuch as you have done it to one of the least you have done it unto me"?

A little widowed girl walked in and sat apart from the others; her eyes filled with tears as she listened. I longed to put my arms round her, but she was too high caste to be touched.

Another hour slipped away; the sun was near setting as we turned homewards. On the way the postmaster accosted us and wanted to hear the news in the world. Bhagyamma went on to the tent. While I talked to him a lad arrived breathless. "You are to come to our house."

He led me to a merchant's house where visitors are staying. These turned out to be old friends from elsewhere; the host had called other local friends and prepared a solemn reception. A carpet was spread on the verandah; besides the waiting house party a bazaar crowd collected round the verandah in a moment. "Talk to us on religion," demanded my friends.

If I had been offered a choice I fear I should have missed this opportunity. Since two o'clock we had been at work talking almost ceaselessly. It was now nearing seven. But no choice was given; every eye turned expectantly; and with that the greatness of the chance gripped me.

"You want to hear about religion?" I began. "What, think you, are its marks?" The hallmarks of religion passed in review, and the Figure who bore them all in shining impress painted as best I could. They listened and listened. Never once, when the things He said and did, how He lived, how He loved, how He died, are brought before the people, have I met any opposition, or indeed anything but the consciousness that they were being attracted by Him.

The children followed me home, among them the little widow girl whose wistfulness was so moving, and the son Nursamma wants to see guided into the way of peace.

The children's thoughts were on different lines. One boy in the sandy lane turned a somersault; the rest caught the infection in a moment, and flung themselves earthwards also, till the dust flew up thick, while the glow of the sunset lingering in the sky converted the smothered atmosphere into a golden cloud in which brown bare limbs whirled wildly about a choking missionary to whom till the tent was reached petitions were incessantly presented: "Have you brought a doll this time?" "Will you give me a book?" "I want a picture!"

What *I* want is a school![1]

[1] Extract from a letter sent home in 1926, after I left India, by a missionary visiting this very village:

"I got such a welcome as I never dreamed of. When they heard you had written lovingly of them the women's eyes brimmed with tears; they could not do enough, or say enough, to express their appreciation of our coming; and we heard again the exclamation that is becoming familiar with repetition, 'Would Hindus remember like this?'

"Nanchâri insisted on my having a rest after the fatigue of the journey; she sat by fanning me, for it was very hot. I wanted her to rest herself, but she began to say how our coming had made hunger, weariness, and worry disappear. 'Missiamma,' she continued, 'the Lord sent you here. He knew how we had need of refreshment and comfort. You did not know us, nor we you; you did not come because you love us, but because you love Him and He bade you come. And what I do for you now I do for Him. We are both in Him, and our coming together is a meeting in Him.'

"I could go on all day telling you about them. Surely there was never more sincere Christian fellowship than they made us feel we had with them, though they do not outwardly call themselves Christians."

CHAPTER VI

I AM down in the dumps. The universe is a sodden suet pudding and I a depressed currant in the middle, well caught in its thick and visionless opaqueness.

In a letter from Bukkuru Balamma, the Christian teacher, writes that Sita Ramana has grabbed our new Mohammedan school there. He assembled the Mohammedans of the town and threatened them. It appears they are nearly all of the poorer class; a few are small shopkeepers, tailors, cart drivers, etc., but many of them are servants in Brahmin houses. So it was not difficult for the enemy to cow them and get them to say they wanted him to have the school, and to put their signature to some document he had prepared. Balamma writes that he now goes in and out of the school, and calls himself manager. Mahabub Bi, the Mohammedan teacher, is *gosha*, and retires behind the scenes when he comes in; her father, Ghulab Khan, is frightened of Sita Ramana; Balamma herself says why should she, a Christian, go on helping in a non-Christian school?

The mental atmosphere is murky with the smoke of depression.

* * * * *

A few days later.

> "It may be, in yon smoke concealed,
> Your comrades chase e'en now the fliers,
> And, but for you, possess the field."

How ashamed I am, for news has come that makes that quotation a fulfilled prophecy.

A marvellous movement among the village caste communities has sprung up in a neighbouring district. Whole families and groups of families are asking for the new teaching. The workers amongst them are scarcely allowed time for food or rest; farmers, merchants, all sorts of people, are being drawn in and becoming deeply interested. The missionaries are at their wits' end how to cope with the situation and have asked for help.

So Sita Ramana may have it all his way (except for protests by post) in Bukkuru for the present; the work in Andapur cannot be followed up just now; I am going with Miss Cullum immediately for a tour among those villages where the people are pressing for instruction.

* * * * *

Madduru. Here are Miss Cullum and I having a rest on the tent floor as our luggage carts have not yet arrived, experiencing various joys of camp. The cook went in advance to prepare breakfast for us on arrival; but he seemed unable to obtain *cholum* straw for the bullocks, or firewood, or any supplies at all. But Miss Cullum is one who tackles things in no roundabout way. To every visitor who approaches the tent she gives a clear hail: "Ho, sir! we have no straw for the bullocks, nor grass for the pony, there is no wood to cook with, great hardship has befallen; go to the village officer and tell him we must have straw and wood—go quickly. . . ."

Children were playing in the *tope.*[1] "Ho, children! we have no straw, we have no wood, great trouble has come; go to the village officer . . ." etc.

A passer-by walked near. "Ho, stranger! sir! what is your village?[2] Why don't you answer? We have no straw, we have no wood, great trouble has come, go to the village. . . ."

More children appeared in the *tope.* "Ho, children!"

[1] Small wood, or plantation of trees.

[2] The usual inquiry of strangers, instead of personal names.

They crowded near, glad to peep inside the tent. "We have no straw, we have no wood. . . ."

I had lain there highly entertained; but exerted myself now to croak out, "Go, children! collect some sticks and bits; just anything to make a fire with."

With the universal eagerness of children to help they departed, urged on by Cull's, "Yes, go, bring quickly!" In a few moments they returned with an assortment of twigs. "More, more," urged Cull; they came in with further treasures of dry leaves and dry cow dung,[1] holding out their baskets to Cull, who gazed enraptured at the contents. "This is good for food, is it not?"

The missing link in her rapid thought was clear to me; the children, however, gaped at her blankly; were such oddments truly the food of the white people?

"Good for the cooking of food," I gasped when I could speak, and trust that our reputations were saved.

A friendly village woman who had been standing at a distance for a long time now took courage to come nearer. "Teach her something," Cull commanded, and obediently I sat down with her in a corner of the tent to teach her something. "Oh, how beautifully you speak," said Cull afterwards; "how that woman listened to you; now she won't forget that story."

Next day, midday. "Here is that woman again," said Cull. "There now, see how you impressed her, I think she wants to learn more."

Highly gratified, I beckoned the woman near.

"You remember the words of yesterday?" I asked kindly.

"Everything, every word, I have forgotten nothing."

It was hard not to swell visibly. "Tell me what you remember."

"We have no straw, we have no wood, great trouble has come, go to the village. . . ."

[1] A commonly used fuel.

I retreated in a hurry.

But this morning things were no laughing matter. In Madduru there is a street whose inhabitants permit no low caste person ever to pass through. Indeed they would like to forbid us Europeans. A peculiar sect of Brahmin Vaishnavas live there; they intermarry only among themselves, i.e. in that street; they are superior to the rest of the world. Cull is rather bent on gaining an entrance; but last time they would not allow her to sit down for a moment anywhere. We resolved on another attack this morning.

The Biblewomen started early; I hoped they had gone to the general bazaar; but to my dismay I found Radha in full swing in that very street. I could hear her voice raised, evidently in some excitement; angry retorts were buzzing round; the place was rapidly becoming aflame. The plan had been for Cull and myself to arrive alone to a quiet normal street. But here we were now; the street full of angry, contemptuous people, all wearing Vishnu's trident on their foreheads and looking awe-inspiring enough! Zeal and enthusiasm are Radha's strong points, but hardly tact and conciliatoriness. The other Biblewoman looked a little scared, for every moment more Vaishnavas with that ferocious-looking trident were streaming out from the houses, and I felt my courage oozing out from every pore.

"*Amma*," I began with a quailing heart, turning to a woman on a *pial*.

"Walk on, walk on," said the woman, "why do you stop here? Go on," wafting us off her sacred street with the customary gesture.

"I am a stranger here," I said. "We have walked from over there in the heat; you can see how hot we are; is it the custom here to say to tired strangers 'Walk on, walk on'? I see you all have the marks of piety in your face; indeed I have heard you are all great *bhaktas*; [1] but now I have come

[1] Religious devotees.

to see you you just say 'Walk on!' Is it a mark of *bhakti*?[1] Where I come from we think quite different things marks of piety. May I tell you a story about it?" Eventually their attention was won to some extent.

"She told you to walk on in ignorance," said an old man. "Your words are true."

That street is more penetrable and penetrated than it knows. In the village school where presently we distributed leaflets, the sons of the sacred street took them with great eagerness. The schoolmaster brought a friend whom he introduced as a great *pundit*, and added softly, "And a secret Christian like myself." We learned that he was an inmate of that very street. "Every day in my house I read the Bible," he confessed. This *pundit* and the schoolmaster, and another Hindu, besides the catechist (who is himself a caste convert) and another caste Christian, came presently to the tent; some hours were spent in intimate talk about Christianity. Later on others joined; it was truly delightful to find so many of the chief people either Christians or on the verge. All day long people were with us; and now as I am writing by the glimmer of the moon we are waiting for some young widows eager to pay a visit.

Next day. Not much waiting had to be done—before we had eaten a hasty dinner a whole crowd of women turned up. This *tope* is a mile from the village; the women have worked in the fields all day, and as we particularly wanted a quiet talk with the widows we let it be understood no one else was to come; but the moment it is whispered that someone is going to the tent, the others will not be stopped. There they sat in the moonlight and we started our meeting. It is good to speak to people so eager to listen; yet I cannot honestly say there is less earnest attention in our own district. Only here it seems to come to something and there it does not—that is, as far as outward

[1] Religious devotion.

building up is concerned. Long past midnight we got to bed.

Next day the same eager interest met us. When we went to a village Gangana, the schoolmaster, sent the children away from school that he himself might have the chance of asking all he wished about Christian truth. The deep interest and struggle that is going on around is most impressive. From a village near, another schoolmaster came to the tent; he is baptized, but still the ways part in front of him. Much persecution has he bravely endured before at last his family tacitly accepted his loss of caste. Now he is urged to leave his post in the Government educational service; for he is desperately wanted as an evangelist, and has great gifts for it. But he is halting. His family tolerate him as a Government teacher, but would have none of him as a public Christian preacher. All the hot noon hours these men were in our tent; we read through Hebrews xi. with them; one thing led to another. Paget's sermon on "Double-mindedness" and G. Adam Smith's on "Overcoming" came to my mind and gave me what to set before them. They came again in the afternoon; the sun went down and the moon came up and still they were there. My heart was so drawn out to them and so conscious of terrible problems that I almost broke down. One thinks of the people, sheep without a shepherd, in all the villages round, and here among the men sitting in our tent were those who could make another breach in the wall of caste, helping others to follow with less agony perhaps; one man could be a teacher and guide to many, for a little loss of some worldly esteem and property.

"You say all the thoughts in our hearts," they confessed; "you read our minds as through glass." Bless Paget and G. A. Smith for their far-off thinking in Scotch and English studies which here feeds Indian villagers!

Gangana the waverer kept on repeating that he was torn

in his mind; he would come again, he would hear more, he would write. May all good influences be around him! To forswear old loyalties, to follow a new one but faintly discerned, that is hard. Nor is it any easier in India than in England to renounce money and position for conscience' sake.

* * * * *

Vempalli. We are camped to the east of a great rock; cacti grow in the clefts; from little ledges large owls blink down on us in the sun. A few mango and tamarind trees give shade to our tents; in front flows the small, narrow channel conserving the scanty trickle of river water. Beyond is the wide river bed, now only burning stretches of dry sand.

A tiny temple perches on a ledge of rock above us; steps hewn in the stone lead up to it; and the smoke of the priest's holy cooking purifies the air (according to him!). A tall gaunt woman who looks almost sexless stalks grimly about, saying "Siva! Siva!" every time she mounts the steps; she is the priest's servant. Yesterday she joined the group of women to whom we were reading and explaining a chapter in St. John's Gospel. I felt a little nervous that she might interrupt or scoff, but, instead, she addressed us as "*Maha talli*,"[1] and listened with great interest. When someone else interrupted she said impatiently, "Be quiet! let *her* talk!"

I am writing under difficulties; a group of people is sitting near and desires "words," but without cessation I have been talking for three hours to successive groups—now here are still more people. We have not had in Vempalli in these three days a single minute's rest during the day, except for hasty meals. I confess to relief that the moon is now too old for night meetings. Instead, Miss Cullum and I have long confabs, comparing methods, habits too,

[1] Great Mother. A term of respect.

and are nothing if not frank! To-day I took off her way of conducting a meeting for the Christian *Mala* women. She has been a teacher so long that meetings are apt to be of the nature of classes where orderliness is of prime importance. The women, however, have to bring their babies, and babies are obstinately disorderly, especially when they have not drunk but desire to; children also are irregular in their movements; a woman shoots out an arm to hold down a fidgety child; however good the intention the movement disturbs Cull. The women began to feel they should concentrate on sitting still; when questioning time came they had reached a satisfactory state of paralysis. Yet, mentally, they were expected to be fairly nimble. " In a town there was a wedding," Cull began to-day—without the faintest preamble such as " Now I will ask you about the life of Christ "—" What was the name of that town ? "

" Cana," replied a genius in the audience. " Vempalli," she might have said. But this quick-witted daughter of Eve had grasped the missionary groove!

" What a tease you are," gasped Cull when she had finished shedding tears of laughter after my heartless mimicry. But she got back some of her own. " *You* like things comfortable," she said in her not-mincing-matters way; " when we arrive in camp you want a chair and a cushion."

I plead guilty. Walking, or driving in the springless carts, mile after mile over rough tracks, I find exhausting to the head and back of Brother Ass. Cull, on the other hand, comes out as fresh as a lark. The people are waiting to greet her, and she wastes no time in rest before responding and starting in. " How much have you learned since last time ? How many new stories ? How many lyrics ? "

I am certainly learning this, to give other people their regular row to hoe—they have things finely organized here.

Reddipalli. To-day we had our little share of tribulation. Planning to be off by sunrise we arose at 4.30 a.m.; tents were struck and packed, but though all was ready by six o'clock the carts failed to turn up. We sent again and again; at last at nine o'clock they rumbled up. We climbed into ours and were moving off when a great crying arose behind us. "Come, they are quarrelling!" We looked back and saw Miss Cullum's Lascar and a Mohammedan cart driver at each other's throats. The Lascar seemed to have the upper hand, and was about to heave a great brick on the Turk. Cull came on like a whirlwind and seized the brick. But even as she talked peace something seemed to enrage the man afresh, and snatching a big tent peg he went for the other. Being a low caste man and the other a Mohammedan, catastrophe seemed imminent, for co-religionists stood ready immediately to take sides; Cull simply seized his arm and prevented the first blow. Meanwhile I had ascertained the cause of the quarrel, which was that one more cart had come than had been ordered—a very easy misunderstanding owing to the many messages. "We'll have the extra one, too," I said. "The Biblewomen will be less crowded." That removed the original cause, but not the evil spirit now on the scene; we dared not leave till every bit and bundle had been loaded up and all the carts could start together.

It had been a horrid occurrence,[1] and Cull and I sat in our cart feeling rather upset. What to do with that bloodthirsty Lascar?

"This takes it out of me more than three days' work," said Cull, "and I don't know what to do with Bassappa."

"Let's ask," I said in a matter of fact way. "There's wisdom somewhere, and we might get it."

Cull grunted. "I don't feel like praying."

"Nor I," I admitted. "Let us tell God we are too cross to pray, but that we need wisdom all the same. I am not

[1] In all the years of camp life since I never met a repetition.

going to wait till I have on Sunday clothes inside when I know I am in need."

"I feel more peaceful now," said honest Cull after we had carried out our resolve.

I am writing all this in the sweltering noon; this time the tents are pitched in scarcely any shade; the glaring plain quivers with heat; now and then a wind from the infernal furnaces springs up and scorches me dry; it dies down and I don't know which state is the more trying. I can hear Radha preaching under a tree; nothing wears down her enthusiasm. There, she has just come in and said, "The women want to see you. I told them my Missiamma has a Telugu mouth, and her coming is as the coming of a heavenly messenger."

"Are you not likely to die of pride in your Missiamma?" I asked.

But Radha is not to be caught out. With the same simplicity she continued, "*You* don't bear the heat as Miss Cullum does! She sits down in the houses and says nothing. *You* say, 'Let us sit outside in a little wind!'"

I hide a diminished head. How they notice!

* * * * *

We divided forces. Cull, despising all hardship, went with the Biblewomen, but without a tent, to the "Village of the Shepherds," whence urgent messages came not to pass them by. She will spend the night in such accommodation as the village offers; I envy her capacity of sleeping through most kinds of noises, upon which Radha also passed admiring remarks, openly disparaging my inferiority.

The path to the village where I was bound led through a *cholum* field ripe for harvest; a woman was keeping watch. "What do they call you, *amma*?" I addressed her, in the friendly habit of the Indian road.

"Lakshmi," she answered, a little fearfully; I was alone

and must have been a somewhat inexplicable phenomenon to her. I looked at her face, in which there were lines of sorrow and resignation.

"When you go home to-night, Lakshmi, who will be in the house?"

The simple inquiry after her family opened unexpected floodgates. "Nobody, not a single one; my husband is dead, my son is dead, my daughters are married—far, far away; the house is empty."

"Lakshmi, the house is not empty. When you go home to-night Someone will be waiting."

"No, no one is waiting, that is why I took this post of watcher. I cannot bear the empty house, it is better to be here in the field with the birds."

"Listen, Lakshmi. Someone *is* waiting. He sent me here to tell you so."

Nearly half an hour passed in the *cholum* field before I hurried on, fearing to be late for the women's meeting which had been arranged. I need not have troubled; they had not yet returned from the fields. I sat down by the blacksmith outside the village and began talking to the quickly gathering group, naturally on the thing at hand, their blacksmithing, the heating in the fire, the hammering, the finished article—and the obvious parable. With the simple apparatus just in front the words easily found their way. "This is the teaching for us," said a woman; "Good teaching for me," said another, of whom I learned presently that life had dealt her the hammer-blows of depriving her of husband and son.

At last the women came; in no time the little school-house was filled, while others were still trying to get in; we held our meeting inside while the crowd waited outside, ready for us when we emerged with the familiar phrase, "We desire words of righteousness." So it was dark by the time I reached the *cholum* field again on my return journey;

not expecting to be so late I had brought no lantern, but dimly I discerned a figure in the path in front of me.

" Who is there ? You, Lakshmi ? So late ? Why have you not gone home long ago ? The birds are all asleep."

" Oh I waited, how long I waited! Many hours you did not come. Tell me more."

In the dark we went on together—and did Someone walk with us and take the hand of poor lonely Lakshmi in the *cholum* field and comfort her ? Did a dim perception steal over her that she, the watcher against ill, was herself watched over for good, that goodness and mercy were following even her ?

CHAPTER VII

Bukkuru. Arrived here. These words sound simple enough, but cover a multitude of complications. For long I had been trying to do battle with Sita Ramana; when at last a visit to Bukkuru became possible, rain and still more rain came pelting down. That meant difficulties with carts. Still, one could but try. Carts were ordered to be at the little country station, where I arrived hopefully yesterday midday. No carts were to be seen. It had rained again the night before, and now the sky looked ominously black.

" Every one is ploughing," said the people standing about on the platform. " No one can give you carts; the oxen are all needed for field work."

" Stationmaster, if I cannot get carts to go on may I sleep in the goods shed to-night ? "

" I have no objection. But it is full of bags of chilli and there are more to be put in," was the reply.

My heart sank a little; no means of going on, and if I stayed the company of pungent sacks of chillies all night.

Remembrance, however, of many previous holes in camp, always with a way of escape, proved sustaining, the thought of returning by the evening train was rejected with contumely.

Erana was despatched with instructions to do his utmost to get carts in the adjacent village. Casting apprehensive glances at a lowering sky, I settled down on the platform with a book. Time passed on leaden feet. One hour, two hours. Ha, the creaking of wheels! Erana with a cart!

" *I* chartered this cart," said a merchant, with rows of sacks on the platform, dashing my hopes.

" I did not promise you," said the cart man, raising them up again.

Wild altercation followed. Evidently the cart man did not relish the prospect of the heavy sacks on soft roads, and hire cut fine; he would much rather take my lighter loading and probably greater pay; the merchant also foresaw many difficulties for his grain and clung to his rights, or supposed rights. "I did not take any advance, I did not promise," the driver reiterated. "You did! you word-breaker, you thief! Your cart shall never be hired again by anyone if you take not my bags . . ." thus the angry merchant.

"I did not promise," the cart man repeated stolidly.

"You did!"

In the end I appealed to the trader. "Are your sacks in a hurry?"

"Yes, they are promised for the Bukkuru market."

"But that is not till Monday. Will you not let me have this cart? Another might be obtained to-morrow, or this one will return and still take the grain in time; I have nowhere here to put up."

"I cannot quarrel with *you*!" he replied with courtesy. We began to load, when lo! the jingle of bells; here, after all, two or three hours late, were the carts from Bukkuru. So the merchant got his grain off too.

At nearly five we set off. Then the black heavens could hold themselves up no longer; down, down came the rain, as if it meant to wash the whole district away. I huddled in the cart, thankful for its fairly tight cover. The road became softer and softer, the bulls slower and slower, moving at the rate of one mile an hour now. At last the rain grew lighter and finally stopped; the moon rose over a watery plain. At eight o'clock we reached the banks of a river—a dry sand bed mostly, but now a broad, deep, fast-flowing current. The men waded in to test it; a rider on a horse came by and also ventured in; all turned back. "It is up to a man's armpits," they reported, "the carts cannot cross."

So there we were, in the middle of the wilderness, no shelter near anywhere, not even trees, the sky black and threatening as if it meant to break forth again any moment —I was not yet out of my hole! I slithered down from the cart; the ground was soaking wet everywhere; I was tired and hungry, and as I stood by the moonlit rushing water, meditating on what to do, had to ward off a feeling of lonesomeness.

"Is there a *chuttram* [1] in the village we passed?" I asked.

"No, nothing, it is only a small hamlet."

"Nevertheless, let us go back there," I ordered.

For I had noticed a little temple, and thought if rain came pelting down again it might afford shelter. But alas! it proved a four-walled construction with a securely locked door. There remained the big dripping tamarind-tree and the platform round its base, shining wet.

"Erana, bring my dinner, please," I said composedly, and some cold stringy goat meat and bread made its appearance. My mattress was unrolled in the cart—the bulls munching close by preventing for me any idea of sleep, though not for Erana and the driver disposed on the platform. Near midnight the men thought the river might have run down; we jogged off, I wishing devoutly that the oxen had not eaten all the straw, for a thin mattress proved but a poor buffer. Other carts were at the river which was less broad and deep; we could have crossed easily, but the cart in front, heavily loaded—it was the merchant with his bags—tried to rush the opposite bank, something snapped, and we, behind, were blocked, and stuck in the swishing, swirling water. "Another hole," I thought; but though it took a long time to untie the bulls from carts already over the river and bring them to the rescue of the heavy one, and in turn to mine which was meanwhile sinking deep into the soft

[1] Native rest-house.

bottom, we got safely out in the end. Pursuing our slow and jolting way we arrived here in the early hours of the morning. And so to bed and a short sleep at last.

And now for the battle with Sita Ramana! Here are Ghulab Khan and his daughter, and I shall hear all the news.

Later. Sita Ramana has certainly put, not one finger, but two whole fists into the pie of the Mohammedan school here; in fact he has jumped in bodily. I hear that after the assembly with the Mohammedans he created a school committee, with the *mullah* [1] as president. A system of fees was agreed upon, the fees to come to the committee, not to the teacher who did the work. Old Ghulab Khan was called headmaster and his daughter assistant; each was to receive a regular salary. Since then the school committee have taken all the fees that came, but have not paid one penny of salary! Sita Ramana also called in the Supervisor of the Educational Department, another Brahmin, to see the school; the two Brahmins (so goes the report) came to an understanding in the matter; the supervisor promised recognition of the school and grant-in-aid in eight months' time.

Old Ghulab Khan was in great distress, the interference bewildered him, and certainly the poor man is much the loser! My arrangement with them had been that for the present I paid his daughter no salary, but allowed her to take all the fees; I added a Christian teacher who received remuneration, and who, by increasing the efficiency of the school, made it more attractive, hence more fees! Now for some months they had had nothing, though they had laboured. Yet he was so devoured by terror of Sita Ramana and of the fact that he put his signature to some agreement, that he feared prison if he drew back. It gave me a little insight into Brahmin tyranny to see the cowed old man;

[1] The religious official who sounds the daily calls to prayer.

if they have this effect upon Mohammedans [1] who owe them no allegiance or religious subservience, what will not be the effect upon the "untouchable" classes who owe both! I advised Ghulab Khan to bring this committee along to see me; they are the chief Mohammedans here, and the rest of the community will listen to them.

It is such a heavenly day, after all that rain yesterday, now that the sun has come out everything is golden in an almost intolerable way. The ground is green everywhere, golden green; the light filters delicately through the shining leaves of the great tamarinds surrounding the house; the hillsides near have become green in a night; deep purple cloud shadows rest on them, a foil to the radiant summits. The sky is clear blue, kissed by opaque white clouds; in this sunshine even the manure heaps look picturesque. But the flies! The grease spots on this letter are eucalyptus oil, dropped on it to keep them off. I don't wonder Luther called flies emissaries of hell and threw inkpots at them; I, more modernly, spread fly-papers.

Later. The Mohammedan committee have come and gone. The first round in the contest has gone against Sita Ramana. A new agreement has been signed by Ghulab Khan and the others to the effect (1) that they prefer a lady manager for a school of girls, (2) that the agreement with Sita Ramana is cancelled as no salaries were paid by him as promised, (3) that they solemnly request me to be in charge of the school. A copy of this pact, addressed to the Inspectress, has left by the outgoing post, with the request for speedy recognition of the school. Now we await developments, and meanwhile I went to the bazaar to greet old friends.

On the way to Radha's house a woman accosted me in

[1] In other parts of India where Mohammedans are of good standing economically and socially such Brahminical overlordship would not obtain.

a lane: " You are passing without talking? It is many days!" I sat down on the nearest *pial*; several caste women came to listen. A young woman stood in the doorway.

" I want to learn to read," she said. It appeared she was the owner of the house on the *pial* of which I was sitting. " Who are you, *amma*?" I asked, noting uneasily her profusion of jewellery, and a certain unmistakable manner, " a *Bassavarali* [1]—a servant of the gods?" I added straightly.

It was even so. " I am sorry I cannot teach you to read," I went on, seeing her motive was not desire for good or for knowledge, but for added attractiveness in evil. " Your way is a bad way."

The respectable women were taking her very calmly, and seemed surprised at my uncompromising attitude. " But what is she to do for a living?" they said in astonishment to me. " It is her livelihood."

" The more shame to this town," I said as I got off the *pial*. The absence of any kind of public standard shocked me afresh. Such absence is a natural and logical consequence of the fact of prostitution being connected with temples, with religion, with the whole system of Hinduism of which it is a recognized part.

The merchant women asked me into their house—two old schoolgirls lived in it. One, now at a distance, had just become a widow.

" You will write to her and try and comfort her?" I said to the sister.

" I shall not write to her," was the reply.

" Why not?" I asked in amazement.

" We must not write any letters," she answered.

" Not one sister to another in such great trouble?" I asked incredulously.

" No, we are not allowed to send any letters," she repeated.

[1] Temple servant, i.e. prostitute.

"Of all the tyrannies——" I began in indignation, but soon checked myself. This, too, is part of India's thought of women, still regnant in this out of the way corner.

It has already altered elsewhere; education is bound to effect it. Such changes, however, come very slowly. Is there no way of hastening them?

Meanwhile, poor Parvati is left unreached in her desolation by the sympathy of the sister who wept as she thought of her. I mourn more than ever the loss of our Hindu girls' school here. By means of it surely little rays of light would be penetrating the obscurantism in Bukkuru.

* * * * *

Here my Mohammedans returned again. They say that though they will help all they can, the school must not continue to be held in Ghulab Khan's house; it is small and dark, and the temptation too great for Mahabub Bi to be ever after her domestic matters. They would show me a better house.

Later. As I was departing to see it Mr. George Pillay, the doctor, called, and related that Sita Ramana is on the warpath. He goes about the town declaring he is manager of the Mohammedan school, and flourishing in proof some official paper with the stamp of the Educational Department. Now what can that paper be? There was further information about him which distressed me greatly. As he paid no salaries the decent teacher of his school left. A woman known to be his mistress has taken the vacant place. Alas! I had given him credit for being clean in life and purpose; but now it seems he is unscrupulous in every way. To think that my little Soni and other Telugu schoolgirls dear to me have now as their only teacher Sita Ramana's mistress; that the educated Hindus of the town calmly send their daughters to be taught by a woman of bad character. No voice is raised in protest. The desperate need of decent public standards!

Two days later. Things here are like a kaleidoscope; hardly is a matter settled and I dare to breathe freely when a little shake of the fates upsets everything again. I went with the Mohammedans to see the house they offered; it lay at the end of the town farthest from the Mohammedan quarter. I declined it, then another man praised up his proffered accommodation. It proved to be in the main bazaar street—the *gosha* teacher would never be able to get to and fro. For the moment no other way out offered; we all went back to the present school-house. There it occurred to me how it might be altered, and made into a separate school- and dwelling-house. With this proposal every one seemed pleased; but a whole day went in negotiations, drawing up an agreement, specifying measurements, materials, advance to be given, the time limit, etc., for the proposed alterations. I went to sleep on a signed agreement with Ghulab Khan. Then it poured with rain all night. As a result another deputation arrived in the morning. "Ghulab Khan is sitting weeping; the rain has come again; no one can make bricks; how can he finish within the time? But we have thought; we will show you yet another house."

We went to see this house. To my delight I found that it would do if more windows were put in. Over this building estimate began a fresh palaver of some hours. They, naturally, sought their own advantage; I also wished it to be of advantage to them, for it is a solid tie! Let by all means their interests and those of the Mission be bound together—only, too far on their side I will not go! Hence, time and still more time was required, and patience and still more patience. A trickle of humour helped. They spoke Hindustani among themselves, but Telugu with me, concluding I knew no Hindustani; but my holiday lessons enabled me to gather at least the gist of their private consultations. "Shall we take so much? Shall we ask for more?" My longing to share the joke at last overcame me, and I mimicked their greediness, "Shall we take so much?" A general burst of laughter brought us all a little humanly near, and the negotiations to a desirable end. Another agreement was signed and witnessed, more satisfactory than the old. For the leading Mohammedans who clubbed together to buy that house for the school are the signatories; and they are the very men whom Sita Ramana formed into his Mohammedan school committee.

Joyfully the afternoon was spent in the school, practising Hindustani and making friends with the pupils; after closing it was proposed to visit their homes. The whole school came with me *en bloc*. Was it not delightful to trail through Bukkuru again with a crowd of children at one's heels?

Next day. The post arrived and brought the official letter from the Educational Department recognizing me as manager of the Mohammedan Girls' School. The Inspectress, bewildered by the bombardment of letters from two sides, had sent a clerk to inspect the school registers to see if they would help. By a curious fluke—for ordinarily I never sign a school register—I had initialled my name in it when I was first asked to take the school over. This date being several weeks earlier than Sita Ramana's petition was taken as sufficient proof of the falseness of his statement that he had started the school and that I had forcibly taken it from him.

Hard upon the post followed a call from Mr. George Pillay, in utter amazement after having obtained sight of the official paper flourished in proof of our antagonist's official recognition. These were the contents: "With reference to your letter of such a date you are herewith informed that Miss M. L. C. has been recognized as manager of the Mohammedan school." The old fox. His capacity for trading on ignorance is greater than I thought, his boldness and his resources are worthy of a better cause.

He is fairly checkmate now over this school. But I still have an aching heart when I pass the closed doors of our Telugu school, yearning over the children who have now no guide for their little feet.

Thoughts go back to girls of Bukkuru taught in that school when it was ours. There was Nilamma. I remember coming in one day just before inspection, when great excitement prevailed among scholars and teachers alike. Examining the little candidates for promotion I reached the fourth standard, containing alas! only two girls. Early marriage takes most of them away before they get so far. Sunny little Adi Lakshmi answered all questions brightly; then it was Nilamma's turn. She stood there looking sulky.

"Read this page, Nilamma."

She gazed at me as if she had not heard.

"Don't you know it?"

Obstinate silence. The teacher came to the rescue. "She gets fits like that when she will not speak. But she will be all right to-morrow in the examination."

So it proved. With flying colours she got her promotion, only alas! to be soon removed from the school for her marriage.

On a subsequent visit Radha took me to see her. She had been married to the husband of her elder sister, a possible and acceptable procedure as there were no children by that first marriage. But I felt indignant, for the man was deaf and dumb.

"What a fate for a bright and educated girl," I said to the mother.

"God wrote it so in Nilamma's forehead," she replied easily. More likely the desire to keep all the property in the family, I thought, and turned to the girl herself.

"Well, Nilamma, come here and talk to me," I called.

But with the shy decorum of the newly married wife she remained half hidden behind the door.

"Have you still got your books?" I asked again.

No reply. "Do you ever read them?" Still no reply. "Nilamma, do you remember the prayers you learned at school?" But not a single answer could I elicit. She was evidently the old Nilamma still, with her shyness and perverse silences. Had any good grain found lodgment in her heart in spite of these?

After that I saw her often, on each visit to Bukkuru. I remember one blazing hot afternoon; I was glad to get into the shade of their courtyard. Others crowded in after us, amongst them another old schoolgirl, Subbamma. "Here, Subbamma!" I said to her, "will you read this?" handing her an open gospel. Subbamma had left school early and was now a mother of three, with not much time for books. With many mistakes she stumbled through the page.

"Now you, Nilamma," passing the book on to her. Did old school habits stir, or was it possibly a little human glow "I can do better than Subbamma"? Faultlessly she read a portion.

"You have not forgotten at all!" I cried delightedly, for this was the first time she had condescended to respond in this way. "Then you read sometimes yourself, don't you? And sometimes," I added, "do you remember how to pray?"

But she had broken through enough reserve for that afternoon. She turned to the book and read on silently. "When you come again you must say a blessing over Nilamma's son," said her mother.

That was my last sight of her, sitting there in the sunshine, reading the words of Jesus, her coming motherhood making life full of sunny promise.

On my next visit I heard the end of her story from the broken-hearted mother and sister. "A little son was born

—behold him! After a few days Nilamma got fever. We called in George Pillay, the Christian doctor, and Nilamma put both her hands together and pleaded. 'I am your child; I have learned in your school; make me better.' But his medicine did not help. 'I want to ask Missiamma for a little cap for baby,' she said again. The fever became worse. Then she seemed to know she would not get better.

"And then," the sister broke in, "she said many words. You know that often she would not talk at all. But, in those last days, she talked much. She said high words, some we could not understand. Many times she asked us, 'Pray. Can't you pray?' But we don't know how. We have not been to your school. She would roll over on one side, she was very weak, but she would turn and put her hands together and say words, 'Our Father . . .' and after that more high words; we cannot remember them, they were too high for us. Also 'Lord Jesus—Saviour,' yes, often she said the name of Jesus. Near the end she suddenly sat up on the cot, her face shining. 'There, there,' she said pointing, 'don't you see Him? The Lord Jesus!' Then she sank back and died."

So Nilamma had not come to school in vain. When she went her lonely way into the shadows His rod and His staff, they comforted her.

Thinking of her and of other little ones now growing up in Bukkuru, I want the way open for them to reach these treasures also.

CHAPTER VIII

THERE are times when one wants to sigh with Thomas à Kempis, "Alas! what kind of a life is this, where tribulations and miseries are never wanting; where all is full of snares and enemies? For when one tribulation retreateth another cometh on, yea and while the first conflict yet lasteth on many others come unexpectedly one after another!" [1]

The old monk might have been a modern missionary. For it is certainly true here that while the first conflict yet lasteth another cometh on.

I am writing in my tent and the reason that brought me here is a burdening one; rumours against one of the evangelists were so persistent that notice had to be taken. The district catechist was to meet me here and help with inquiries on the spot.

So far he has not turned up; this afternoon I went alone to the village near by. That seems natural now, but it has taken difficult years to arrive at this result. I recollect the nervousness and apprehension with which I used to visit a village, half wishing myself well out of it, even looking forward to a few hours hence when it would all be over *some* how. How awkward the moments of entering a village were while I waited to see if a group would collect; wanting people to stand or sit not too far so that I might deliver not too nervously, something carefully prepared! There is no anxiety now whether they will suitably collect. The sense of strangeness has gone, for are not their griefs, their sins, their perplexities my own? Substantially, are we not all going the same road? This consciousness of our common need precludes too the old nervous perplexity: what shall I

[1] Book III, Chap. XX.

talk about? At least it is rarer now. As one looks at the people and tries to picture their life and their inner world, noting the lines on their faces, tired faces, anxious faces, resigned and hopeless faces, cross and sullen ones also, indifferent ones, sometimes trustful faces, not infrequently understanding ones, one feels that the riches to be offered to them are immeasurable, and the heart goes out to them by itself.

I stood still by the first person I met and dropped into conversation. Others collected. "Sit here," they said, pointing to the steps of the village rest-house, where they pressed closely round, cuffing some restless children into quiet that no words might be lost. The atmosphere was so reverent and earnest that a suggestion of prayer followed naturally: "We have been thinking about God; shall we ask Him to bless us?" But the moment it was over the inevitable trifler spoiled it. "We have time, we, to sit and pray, have we! What about our livelihood?" came a scoffing voice, and the audience followed the lead. The earnest tone could not be recovered. As no one could read, no leaflets could be distributed. But some of the men remained serious and friendly, and accompanied me back to the tent. It was an exquisite walk towards the sunset. It had rained all round the horizon where clouds were massed, but now in its setting the sun shot through from below these clouds, and the glory was almost painful. Great floods of radiance were poured out lavishly everywhere, over the fields, the distant hills, the wide plains. I paused by a *saddu* [1] stalk in the fields; it grows over three feet high, and the ear is from three to four inches long. This particular *saddu* stalk had its ear, or cob, just bursting its sheath; half in, half out it lay, the leaf still tenderly enclosing it. It moved me deeply. So delicate it was, so motherly, so modest. I held it in my hand reverently and wanted to kiss the lovely miracle. The villagers looked at me astonished, but I think not without sympathy.

[1] A sort of millet.

Perhaps they thought I was making magic over their harvest!

* * * * *

Still Chidananda had not turned up; so again this morning I went to a village alone. On the way spear grass pierced my stockings and pricked badly; prickly burs crept up inside my skirt; a stream had to be waded; at the next one I was for heaving stones in on which to cross; some men in the fields at a distance who were watching left their work to point out a crossing a little higher up—are there any people in the world more courteously ready to help than these friendly Telugu people?

In the village I found people were going out to the fields. Not quite knowing where to make a beginning, I asked for the village officer's house and was shown there. He had gone out but would shortly return. I sat down on the *pial* outside to wait.

"Come inside," a man called, evidently at the mandate of his mistress. For the *Reddi's* wife and other women came from an inner room, and neighbours pressed in from outside.

"Where have you come from? Andapur? What is your work? To say words of righteousness? Will you say some now?"

I said some. I did not stay to hover on the outskirts of soul things. A sense of urgency was on me. The face of the *Reddi's* wife drew me on. Her eager listening did not flag for one moment. Perhaps half an hour or more passed. Suddenly the whole group melted away. In strode the *Reddi.* Then I understood the yearning and hunger in the wife's face, her manifest search for comfort. He had no sign of greeting for the stranger, perhaps he was vexed to see me there. Politely I asked him what day the post reached that village.

"On Saturdays," he said over his shoulder as he walked past.

"I still wish to ask you something," I said to his back. He began divesting himself of his shirt, then sat down half naked and talked to a man near him.

"Are carts to be hired here?" I inquired.

"No."

"But I saw some in the village as I passed. May I ask you kindly to supply me, as you are the village officer?"

"These carts belong to the *Karnam*.[1] He will not give for my asking. He and I are at enmity," was the unwillingly given information.

"I don't wonder," I thought. Anyone more surly in behaviour would be hard to find. As it was his house, and as he evidently wanted me out of it, I took leave, glad that he had been away so long and given me a chance with his wife. Only half an hour, and a lifetime of hunger and loneliness! Her face haunts me now.

Walking through the village I spied a merchant. "You can read?" I asked him. "Yes."

"Would you like this?" offering him a leaflet. He accepted it.

"May I sit in your verandah and read what I have given you to your wife?"

"Yes." I went in where he showed me; he sat down himself in the verandah, the wife stood in the doorway behind; people crowded in and filled up the courtyard. A long time passed in talking to them. The merchant couple were very interested and finally bought books. Among the people who had drifted in stood a man who seemed of better education than the rest. Inquiries elicited the fact that he had studied in the L.M.S. High School in Bangalore. A packet of Gospel stories, parables and psalms was offered to him.

"Will you take these?" I asked. "Could you not teach the people? You say you have read all the Christian Scriptures. Will you not give them what you have received? If you teach them what is written here they could understand it."

"I will, I will," he said readily, taking the packet, and

[1] Official in charge of land records.

I went out into the lane. Presently I approached an old man sitting in the sun on his string cot.

" He is blind," someone said. With the fine sensitiveness of the blind he discerned unusual footsteps, not the patter of bare feet, nor the click of sandals.

" Who is it ? " he asked.

" A teacher of righteousness," said a passer-by who had been in the audience.

" Call her here! " he pleaded. I stood still by his string bed.

" I have come, *ayya*," I said. To my amazement he got off the cot and prostrated himself on the ground before I could prevent it.

" She is not one of our religious teachers," someone explained to him. " She is one of the white people. But our words come to her."

" She teaches righteousness ? " said the old man. " I worship that."

Oh India of the Lord beloved! Precious to her discerning hearts is the spiritual in any form.

" I am old," said the blind man, reseated on his cot. " Soon God will call me. Here I sit and think of Him. I say His name, I meditate on Him. Soon I shall be in His Presence."

" And before you go," I said, " would you like to hear of One who came to reveal God to us ? God, whom you think of so much? It is said He was the very Image of the divine glory. Yet He was a poor man in this world, not richer than these villagers. How then did He show forth what God was like ? "

An audience had gathered again as I sat on the cot of the blind man, who listened eagerly.

" What is the name of that Saviour ? " he asked. " Yesu Pra—pra . . ." He stumbled over the word *prabhu*, meaning Lord.

" Say Yesu *Swami*," [1] I said, " as you know that best."

[1] Another word for Lord.

"Yesu Swami," he repeated, "I will learn that. I will remember. 'Forgive us, save us,' is that what we are to say?"

"He is glad to have heard you," said the neighbours as I walked on; "he is full of piety."

A woman beckoned to me. "What is it, *amma*?" I asked as I went up to her.

"Can you tell me a way," she whispered, "to get children?"

A good deal may be said on that subject which is not for the village street. I invited her to visit my tent. Among the bystanders the words had been heard and evoked reminiscences. "Some years ago, in Taramulla," began a man, "a holy one arrived; all day the villagers sat at his feet. He was a great saint. A man came and asked for the gift of a son. 'Pay me fifteen rupees,' said the saint; the petitioner was a poor man, but he wanted a son so much that he brought fifteen rupees. The holy man went away. To this day the man has no son; but the saint has the fifteen rupees!"

"Stay and teach us more," said the women; "no one teaches us." The old plea, endlessly repeated.

That *Reddi's* wife remains a burden on my mind.

* * * * *

It rained heavily in the night. I awoke to an English landscape. Fine drizzle swept by like just dissolving smoke; the distant hills were lost, the nearer hillocks loomed spectrally through the mist; the trees a little farther off were delicately veiled; all things were blurred in outline, softened, finally shrouded and hidden. I was reminded of Amiel's injunction, "Let mystery have its place in you." The landscape wore an air of reserve, and at the same time of indescribable intimacy. "You and I are alone now," it seemed to say, "and you, what are you?" it added searchingly, forcing an almost disquieting sense of self-realization upon one's consciousness. From the tent I saw people looming along the road, coming into view, disappearing again. In the villages around, to how many is life just this? Out of the unknown, on the scene a short while, disappearing again; not knowing whence, nor whither. Yet into the shrouding mist of ignorance a light was meant to shine.

* * * * *

Chidananda came at last; in the village of the evangelist our inquiries have now been made; we cannot escape the sorrowful conviction that the rumours are based on fact. The trouble has gone on for a long time; it is not a sudden fall which one might think of excusingly, but a deliberate double life. It seems the whole village knew it. Some of the respectable people did not hesitate to put down what they knew in writing with their signatures. It is a terrible disclosure, and of course an awful scandal. In part I blame the system. Yet it arose so naturally. To place an Indian Christian in a town or village which the missionary could not reach very often, there to proclaim the Christian message among the people of that area; what arrangement could be more suitable? The reaction upon the man whose chief occupation would be preaching: the temptations to laziness and shirking after meeting indifference, perhaps opposition; the almost inevitable lowering of standards through the low atmosphere; the lack of stimulus and inspiration caused by isolation from all Christian fellowship; the mental stagnation and consequent deterioration of a person unaccustomed to read and think; the pressure of example in immorality and dishonesty all around—these are not sufficiently taken into account in such appointments.[1] I am aghast at the report we have to send in.

* * * * *

The sun has come out and dried the tent; before more

[1] In most Missions, of more recent years, the appointment in villages of solitary agents whose sole or chief avocation is preaching is much rarer

rain made it too heavy for transport we moved on to a small bungalow. The journey was slow, as the water-courses were all full and gave me a chance to tire of the amusement of pulling my shoes on and off and carrying my cycle across. When I arrived at a brook wider than usual a cart came along full of caste women, resplendent wedding guests on their way to a marriage. They stopped and offered me a lift; the driver carried my machine unasked, the bulls knowing their own way meanwhile. I remarked to the women how nice it was to meet such readiness to help.

"Every one will always be kind to those who are kind to them," said a woman; "if you do things for people for nothing people do things for nothing for you." Was she not a real philosopher?

On arrival here I settled down to a pile of letters in the verandah, with occasional glances into the green wilderness of hills surrounding it. The village is hidden from sight; all seems peace, and now—after the rain—paradisaical beauty. But no garden of Eden is left undisturbed.

The bungalow-keeper's wife came—at least I thought, on previous visits, she was his wife—now she poured out a tale of misery and wrong; he had cast her off, after keeping her for four years. She comes of a good farmer caste. When I took the man to task for enticing a woman from her home he excused himself by saying she had first been the station-master's prey.

"Now I have been ill and went for medicine," said the woman.

"She wandered here and there," said the man, "so I sent her away."

These interviews with the separate parties became very heartrending. "Do speak to him!" implored the woman. "I think and think of him and cannot forget him." He, however, had already got somebody else. Is it not a miserable story? I told the woman I would pay her fare to the Rescue

Home in Mysore, but that any other help was impossible. Though I begged her to seize this chance I do not think she wants to go really. She has left—going farther and farther into the far country, I fear.

Marala. I am in a tent again; two Brahmin girls, Subbamma, the young widow and her sister Pullakka, the *Karnam's* wife, have just paid me a visit. Both are acquaintances of long standing. To outward appearances they are the "first ladies of the village," belonging to the only Brahmin family in it and treated with deference by all. But inside that home? Pullakka was married as a child to the elderly *Karnam* in this distant village where she had no companionship, no interests, not even the joys of shopping; for the *Karnam* on his occasional journeys to the *Taluk* headquarters buys their *saris* and jackets. "What he brings is our fate," she said dismally once when we had a feminine chat about clothes. The *Karnam's* moral reputation is none of the best. Children have been denied to Pullakka. What interest does her life hold?

Even worse is the case of poor Subbamma. When I first met her her face wore the bloom of youth and happiness. For she had just been married to a young husband in a neighbouring village and was home on a visit. Then, next time: "Oh, Subbamma, what is the matter?" I exclaimed when I saw her. She looked like a broken flower; all spring, all hope, all youth even, gone out of her face. Yet she was but sixteen or seventeen then. I learned that her husband had died.

"And now," she said pitifully, "when I come, is anyone glad? When I say 'I go' do they say 'Stay'? When I weep does anyone say 'Poor thing!'"

To-day she could not stay long as she had fever coming on; Prema took her home. Radha and Pullakka sat with me in the tent. Then more of Pullakka's troubles came out. For three years she and her husband have not spoken to each other. He is a cantankerous old man, and the marriage was misery from the first. Pullakka looked at me wistfully.

"I want to come to you. If I left him and became a Christian could a case be raised against me?"

The poor girl. So she, too, wants to come now. Her sister Subbamma has already begged me many times. Only yesterday evening she said urgently:

"I am of the same mind still as two years ago, but now I want it more. I want to learn; I should like to be a Christian, anyway I must get away from here." About her deep desire she will talk to no one, not even to her sister. They do not seem intimate enough with each other for such confidences. Each sister has now come separately with the same request, "I want to come to you."

What a hard way it is we have to point them. Pullakka's husband is not cruel, nor does he affront her by keeping another woman in their house; her state, though difficult, was bearable. To want to become a Christian because one wished to escape trouble was not a sufficient motive, I explained to her; one must come, compelled by entire loyalty to Jesus Christ. "If you were happy here would you want to come?"

But there is at any rate this step gained: the affection and confidence of these two girls; the fact that they have the sense that there is a refuge somewhere. That they feel they can always turn to Christians is surely something from these reserved and proud people.

Radha told me afterwards that Pullakka's reputation in the village at one time was none of the best. Little wonder. The very attractive and lonely young girl—the very ancient and surly husband. But since our visits, which began three years ago, she had taken our words to heart and lived blamelessly. That also surely is something.

I settled down to my Hindustani grammar in the middle

of the day; the air was intolerably heavy and still; the eye-flies and the mosquitoes (the nasty speckled kind) settled everywhere, stung everywhere; preventive oils and fans seemed quite ineffective; the heavy air seems to give them exuberance of vitality and viciousness. I felt myself getting nervy and irritable, and resolved to throw away Hindustani and try a visit to the village. Perhaps I could catch the *Karnam.* Something must be done for Subbamma. Being a widow her case differs from Pullakka's.

I found him, and privately in their garden I pleaded with him, being the head of the family, to let Subbamma go and study. I cited the example of Penuroy Menakshi. I told him of other Brahmin widows now learning at Andapur; I tried to make plain to him how it was not enough to give a woman rice, she wanted something for her heart, some purpose in life; but I do not think this side entered his understanding at all.

"If she went, what good?" he answered. "Is teaching to be done by Brahmins?"

I fear I blazed a little then. "God Himself can make no greater work for a human being than to direct the souls and minds of little children! Is your measuring of land and fixing of boundaries and keeping records about them a 'great' work? It has to do with the means of life only. But teaching has to do with life itself, with growing souls—which is greater? The doubt is not whether such work is fit for Subbamma, but whether Subbamma is fit for so high a calling; yet let her try and train herself."

The *Karnam* was dumb for a while; a friend sitting by said in a surprised way, "True words." No definite permission could be exacted. As far as I could judge the *Karnam* remained stolidly obdurate; coming back to his first words, "It is not agreeable to us."

"Think it over," I pleaded; "do not decide at once, it is worth considering."

I do not blame the *Karnam* overmuch. The Jerusalem of recognizing the greatness of the teacher's and educator's calling is hardly built yet even in England's green and pleasant land. Perhaps with the *Karnam* the seed will sink in. If not, will Subi have to be helped to leave her home secretly and go to Pandita Rama Bai's Home, or a similar institution ?

The *Karnam* went away; the girls and their old mother came forth from inner rooms and we talked in the little garden. They pressed on me all the dishes they could cook; would not I eat this and that ? But as their food is generally very rich I thought it wiser to ask leave to forgo their gift. Finally they brought some broad beans, ready for their own supper, " Don't you eat these ? "

" Oh yes, thank you."

They insisted on giving me great handfuls. But friendly and intimate as the scene was, it brought its hurt.

" Teach that Subi some sense! " said the mother, " she is often disobedient; she must be punished."

" She is unhappy," I pleaded, " and often not well." Subi suffers a great deal from headaches. I think she is a bit lazy, and I can well imagine she might be sulky. Her sister Pullakka is quite different, a little woman of the world who says the affable thing and has pleasing manners.

" Take Subi away and feed her, who wants her ? " the old woman went on.

Her own mother! And before the girl! Greatly distressed, I glanced at Subi; but she was evidently used to such speeches. " In my mother's house, in my mother-in-law's, it is always the same," she said listlessly.

I took the opportunity to inquire her age, casually, of the mother. " Eighteen." So, according to Indian law, she is no longer a minor. If she left home no legal proceedings could be taken against her or us.

Both girls followed me to the potter's house where Prema

lives and sat in the room while we held the prayer-meeting —they always come to these.

"Salaam, *many* salaams!" Subi said in her old affectionate way when we parted for the night. May God find some way out for this lonely child.

This morning Prema and Radha asked what village we should visit. I spread out the map. "Uppapalli looks within walking distance; I have never seen it, shall we go there?"

On reaching Uppapalli we sat under a banyan tree and started a lyric. Women stopped to listen; one remarked, "We know that one."

"Where have you heard it?"

"Naramma sings it. She tells stories too."

"What stories?" we asked.

"Very beautiful ones. How the son came back again. How the sick were healed."

"Who is Naramma?"

"'Singing Naramma' we call her. She learned in a school. Here she comes."

There she came, hurrying joyfully towards us, an old Bukkuru schoolgirl, now married and on a visit to relations in this village. None of us had known she was there; and I had not seen her since her school days. She sat down with us on the little platform, vigorously joining in the lyric and beckoning to women she knows to come and listen. Her help in the singing was no small boon; for Prema has very little voice, Radha's singing is middling, mine ditto, and the combination execrable, for she wobbles into many keys whereas I attempt to keep to one and the result, even to their ears, must be far from attractive. Yet they beg for more! Naramma collected a great crowd of women, all eager to learn the lyrics from the new book we left with her. At midday she came to Marala, and in the privacy of the tent I learned her story.

They are *Boyer* people, a caste of farmers and coolies, not great on education. But as they lived in Bukkuru Naramma joined other girls and came to our school. Not for long alas! she had barely reached the third standard when the family moved to a village. No more schooling for Naramma. She kept her precious dolls and school books and had happy hours with these treasures. The time came for her to be married. Then something dormant in her seems to have waked up and caused her to revolt. She ran away to Bukkuru to find Radha and ask her where Missiamma was, to whom she would go for further learning. But, alas! Missiamma was away on furlough in England, and no other woman missionary in Andapur. Radha did not know what to do, and advised the girl to go quietly back home and submit to her people's wishes and serve God in her new home.

It was a bitter disappointment to the child. But no other way opened. She returned to be married. Captain of her little soul, however, she remained. Circumstances should not conquer her. Those few short years in the Mission school had left indelible memories. The habit of prayer was continued. Her books were still read, her lyrics sung over and over again. Her people were kind to her, evidently somewhat impressed by her unusual ways. First she taught her mother to pray, later on her husband. Family prayers became an established custom. Neighbours drifted in to hear the singing; story-telling followed, the few stories she could remember. It seems there is always a willing gathering for singing and praying and " words of righteousness " now wherever she is. How impressive her visit to this village had been was revealed this morning. In her own family, to judge from the words of her father and uncle who accompanied her, she seems to be regarded as a sort of religious teacher.

At the beginning of this tour there seemed much reason to mourn that our labour was vain. But to-day, hearing Naramma's story, there is a glimmer as of dawn.

CHAPTER IX

About twenty miles north of Andapur lies the town of Ramidi on the banks of the Parnam river. It has often been on my mind. Now and then evangelists preach in its weekly market, but of organized Christian effort among its busy population there is nothing. Would not a girls' school there be a good thing ? But how to make a start ? I have never been in the place, and do not know anyone there. Why not taste the joy of pioneering ? With the courage of the ignorant I set out single-handed one fine day for the conquest of Ramidi.

The only train left Andapur at noon and an hour later deposited me on the little Ramidi platform. There my troubles began. White and glaring the dusty road showed beyond the station towards the town, two miles away. Not a tree, not a bush for shade. In this broiling midday heat it would have been unwise to walk. There were carts, with the drivers of which already other travellers were chaffering. Hastily I called one. But Ramidi knows no white persons except officials who are always accompanied by a retinue of servants. Here stood a white woman alone—no great catch as a fare, no luggage, no servant, or any other sign of dignity. However, she was white, so she might pay double or treble. They tried it on accordingly, and finding me making a good guess at normal fares, became uncivil—a new experience for me! A compromise was effected in the end, and away I jolted. "Where to ?" asked the driver. Yes, where to ? "To the town," I said vaguely. When we had reached it I scrambled out, he drove off and I eyed the promised land. Glittering in the yellow sunshine the houses and streets lay before me; as I entered the narrow lanes another sense also was strongly assailed. As the town lies on the river bank sand is everywhere; fine dust and grit filled the air and carried impurities; I thought I had never encountered a more malodorous place. These observations were by the way; my chief interest concentrated on people, who returned it tenfold. The women sitting on their *pials* or standing at their doors in the midday leisure viewed me with suspicion; passers-by stared; children congregated at my heels. From door to door I began to be pointed at; some babies screamed at the horrible sight. My heart manifested the proverbial rush towards boots.

> "Was I the first that ever burst
> Upon this staring town?"

"If I don't do something soon," I thought, "I shall find myself turning tail."

But some other part, in this divided kingdom of ourselves, held on grimly and issued resolute commands. "Stand still by those women," it said. "I don't know what to say to them," the other half objected timidly, but obeyed nevertheless. The women regarded me nervously.

"This is Ramidi, is it not?" I said inspiredly.

The women, who had been about to flee into the interior parts of the house, gazed in astonishment. "Our words come to her!" they burst out to one another. "They come," I admitted composedly. "You are Balji caste people, are you not?"

"Yes. Where do you come from?"

"Andapur."

"What do you want here?"

"I thought, perhaps," I ventured, "you would like your girls to learn to read? There is no school here for girls, is there? Would you like one?"

"*Abba*,[1] no. What should girls want reading for?"

"When the women learn reading the men in the house die," chimed in another voice.

[1] An expression of dismay.

Suspicion of me drifted about and condensed. Hastily I dropped the subject of girls' schools. "Boys learn to read here, don't they?" I tried again, refusing the position of an outsider to which the general feeling seemed to relegate me. "Can you read, little brother?" I asked a boy beside me; for by this time the children had crowded close up. "I can! I! I!" came a chorus.

"Then read this; can you?" handing out a leaflet. "A sower went forth to sow," began a clear young voice. I listened myself and began to embellish the story as others listened with me.

"It had been raining," I contributed. These people who know drought became interested.

"Their river was quite full—not like this one," I went on.

Disapprovingly we gazed at the mile-wide stretch of sand representing the Parnam river.

"It was never like this," I warmed to the subject, "it always had water."

"Ah, a living river," said a man who had stopped to listen.

So that is a living river! I mentally registered. A river that always has water. Commend me to non-Christian India for teaching one to understand the Bible. "Go on, brotherling," I said, feeling myself getting astray.

"And as he sowed some seeds fell by the wayside," recited the proud lecturer.

"That was the footpath," I explained. "It led from their village to the next one. I saw one like that branching off from the station road. Where does it go to?"

"There, to the village under that hill," my thirst for information was satisfied.

"And the birds came," went on an impatient little voice.

"Like that!" I called, pointing. A little farther down the street someone had spread a blanket on the ground and on it grain to dry in the sun. The watcher, overpowered by curiosity, had come to join our crowd. Fowls of the earth and birds of the air were having a rapid feast. An angry woman had run out to shoo them away and was vituperating the miscreant watcher, who returned crestfallen to the post of duty.

The recital went on more smoothly now, though I could not forbear comments. "The thorns were prickly pear. They had not cleaned their field well." All round Ramidi this cactus abounds, and as the trouble of clearing land of that pest is very great, the audience beside me in the street wagged understanding heads.

"And the stony ground—you see he had ploughed too near that hill," I asserted, pointing to the low hill scarred by water runnels and broken by jutting rocks, rising immediately beyond some fields north of the town. "The rock extended below the earth surface, there was hardly any soil. That is why things could not grow there. Now read farther down here, little brother," I went on, pointing to the explanation of the parable. "You must understand there is a deeper sense to that story. Care of this world, and the deceitfulness of riches, for instance, is anything known about that in Ramidi?"

"Yes, a great many merchants left the town," someone remarked, "their living failed."

"We must do our cooking now," came from the women of the house; but still they stood listening as the meaning was enlarged upon. "These are good words," they commented.

"Would you not like to read the story again for yourselves?" I asked, offering the leaflet.

"We cannot read." They drew back, a little afraid I was handing them magic.

"It is a pity," I mused. "Would not teaching girls to read be a good thing after all? Yes"—to the boy reader—"you may keep the story."

"We must go to our cooking now," said the women again. I took the hint and passed on. As it was yet early in the afternoon the real reason probably was a little nervousness at this strange invasion of their doorstep and a desire to end it. By the next group I paused again, and then by another, till the sense was gained that the street presented a more friendly atmosphere. Still I had entered no house.

There was, however, a good deal to learn in the street. In a lane I saw a dead donkey, millions of flies on it, and exuding a pestilential odour. The sanitary authorities in Ramidi are slack, I gathered. This was confirmed as I came upon a well, simply a deep hole with no railing or parapet to guard it, in an open space where several lanes met. Children were playing near.

"A little one might easily fall in," I said in concern.

"A great many fowls have fallen in," said the passers-by with equanimity.

"It would need only a few stones to guard it," I suggested.

"Who will take that trouble?" was the callous reply.

Ramidi needs a little education in citizenship, I reflected. This is a disgrace to the British *Raj*. Some underling is at fault.

As I turned a corner a worse sight awaited me. My sense of smell told me I had come near a toddy shop. "What, here, in the midst of private dwelling-houses?" I thought indignantly. "It is supposed to be outside the town." But there unmistakably it was, and here were its clients. A man was just coming out, carrying a small vessel full of toddy, and sat himself down in the lane to enjoy it, every now and then giving a sip to his little boy of three or four.

"Oh, don't give it to the child," I exclaimed; but he laughed and pointed to the shed in the courtyard where sales were going on. A woman sat there with a little one in her arms, and kept on forcing sips on the baby.

"Why not?" she said easily to my remonstrance. "He sleeps well after it, and gives no trouble."

"That well shall be fenced, that toddy shop shall be removed, the streets shall be cleared of insanitary filth," I registered resolves; "though how, I don't know. I have it—we must have a boys' school too! There we might train the future citizens. What schools are there here?" I inquired of the next passer-by.

"There is the Board school, and Narainappa's school, and Varada Raju's, and Venkata Raju's, and a lot more," I was told, and my heart sank. What room was there for another?

The sun was getting lower; wandering about the streets I came upon a private school kept in a verandah. The teacher was chatting with friends in the street, while the school was in charge of one of the bigger boys who stood by the black-board pointing to a word with a stick and shouting it; blithely the whole floorful of thirty or so wriggling infants yelled it after him. Though my advent galvanized their efforts into the delight of showing off, some of the little chaps were weary. "Why don't you send them home?" I said to the teacher.

"There is light yet," was the reply. Yes, that is the idea, from sunrise to sundown the little fellows must be at school; the parents will have it so; do they not pay four annas a month to the teacher to give their child learning, and a meal sometimes also? Let alone presents at festivals. While day-light lasts, therefore, they must get their money's worth out of him; as for the boy, why of course the longer he sits at school, the more quickly he will learn.

Cattle were coming home, trampling the sand in the streets into an intolerable atmosphere; chillies and all kinds of strong spices from the open stalls in the bazaar mixed with it; cooking odours from the houses added to its choking-ness; but the sky, calm and red and gold, overarched it all and held out unfailing promise.

"Will you come into my house for a little?" said a courteous voice at my ear in English.

I turned in surprise and saw a well-dressed Indian standing by me.

"I am the Overseer here, of the D.P.W.[1] I saw you going about in the streets; I think you must be a missionary? I know some missionaries elsewhere, and I greatly respect them. I know you seek our people's good. Please come in and rest a little."

Delighted and thankful, I followed him and sat down for the first time that afternoon. "How long have you been here?" I asked.

"Six months. This is an awful place. I cannot ask my wife to come here. I have to go out to camp a good deal, and cannot take her, neither could I leave her here alone. There would be no companionship at all. And there is a great deal of drunkenness in Ramidi; drunken people go about at night, molesting people; she would be scared."

"Yes, I noticed lack of order in various ways," I replied. "What is the Union doing? Who is the Chairman?"

"A merchant. He can hardly sign his own name."

"But what about the official work—the correspondence with Taluk and District Boards? That is all in English."

"He does not know a word of English. The clerk writes, and the chairman signs. He does not care about anything in the town, only the emoluments of the office. He bribed people to elect him. He gets any amount of bribes now! So does the clerk. This place is full of factions. The chief ones are Hindus and Mohammedans, and these again are all split among themselves. At times the main sections unite against one another; then riots follow. This is the one place in the Andapur District where riots frequently occur. It is

[1] Department of Public Works.

a bad place for epidemics too. We are too close to the river. When it is in flood every one takes the water, and yet all kinds of filth are thrown into it. When cholera is about we get it badly. Yes, there is a Police Station here with a Sub-Inspector; there is a sub-official of the Forest Department too; but I cannot tell you all the bribery and corruption that is going on. It is a hell of a place. I want to get a transfer. What is it that you are doing here ? "

" I want to try and establish a girls' school," I replied.

" That would be excellent. I am glad you are taking an interest. The town needs some good influence badly! I will help you all I can."

" Thank you very much," I said warmly. " If you would inquire about a suitable house I could rent ? "

" Willingly," he promised. " And whenever you come here please come to my house. I shall be glad if you will consider it yours."

With real cordiality we parted. I walked back the two miles to the station tired but rejoicing. I had found a friend, a foothold in the friend's house, a prospect of openings on one hand; and on the other, an overwhelming need. On the whole, I reflected, as I unpacked my supper basket on the platform and waited for the train which would bring me back to Andapur at midnight—it had been an afternoon to encourage anyone to take to pioneering.

* * * * *

Next time I visited Ramidi I took the cycle to circumvent the greed of cart drivers. But now it was the weather which treated me unkindly. Though fine at Andapur, at Ramidi a sudden storm threatened; when I reached the town down came the rain. To lead about a forlorn and dripping cycle in muddy and empty lanes seemed no kind of a prospect; I looked for a refuge. Outside the town is the market-place, a great sandy enclosure, containing the long row of roofed stalls for the protection of wares and vendors on market days. Thither I hastened. I found it crowded with boys, sitting decorously in two long lines, teachers were striding up and down the space in between, and at the far end I beheld an official sitting in state at a table, surrounded by deferential clerks and headmasters. It turned out to be the School Inspector who, to save the trouble of going from school to school, had ordered the inspection of all to take place here in the market; this was now going on.

I stood at the farthest end where the lowest infants fizzled out into space; sheltered indeed from the rain, but feeling forlorn enough. Enviously I looked down the long rows of boys, at the teachers, at the Inspector, all so sure of their ground, so rightly in their places—everybody had their niche, everybody belonged here, only not I. The calling of pioneers who have no connection, no foothold, no rights, lost its attractive hue as I stood there, wishing for some friendly presence.

But that other part in the aforesaid divided personality kept up an unshakeable resolve. "We shall win influence and affection in Ramidi yet," it promised me, chasing dismal doubts. "The rain is stopping, now we will see the friendly Overseer."

He had fever and was in bed. But that did not prevent him from receiving me with a warm welcome and discussing possibilities. I learned what schools there were. There is amongst others a little boys' school kept by a trained teacher called Naraina; he might not be averse to forgo the independence and insecurity of a private school for the security of a regular salary; that is, he might transfer the managership to the Mission. Another man called Venkata Raju taught girls as well as boys in his school; if he would transfer it would immediately mean the beginning of a good girls' school. When inspection was finished the Overseer kindly sent for these men with whom he had some preliminary talk, while I began my street wanderings again. He told me afterwards the prospects were hopeful.

* * * * *

I have now been six times to Ramidi, twice with transfer forms in my pocket, and each time came away disappointed. In Venkata Raju's case the boys' school stands in his father's name, his signature is required. But he is ill and cannot attend to business. Naraina declares his willingness to hand over his school *if* the other does the same. Pioneering, evidently, is not his line. The Overseer thought he could persuade the old father to affix his signature. Yesterday he wrote that all were ready for the transfers; I collected my forms again and was off to Ramidi.

* * * * *

Alas for my beautiful chickens! The fates have nabbed all my eggs. Frightened at the last minute, Naraina decided not to give his school to us. Blow number one. Venkata Raju was prepared to give his. I went to his house with the transfer form. But no. His readiness to transfer resolved itself into a determination to have salary guaranteed for his father as well as himself; an impossible proposition, for the old man is beyond work.

After these many palavers I stand again at the beginning, not one foot advanced, the only plan now being to start a girls' school independently. The next thing therefore is to look round for a good Christian teacher; the Overseer thinks he can get us a house.

* * * * *

Difficulties grow thick as thistles about my path. A depressing letter came from the qualified teacher who, in answer to my advertisement, had promised to come to Ramidi. His manager had offered him more money to stay and now he wants me to raise my offer and then he will come. Such an unworthy breach of comity is of course impossible. That is the second teacher with whom this has happened. A greater blow is that my helpful Overseer has been transferred. Again I am friendless in Ramidi, though he writes that an *Ediga* [1] man has definitely promised to let us have a house for a school and teacher's residence. Still I am in the blues over that transfer.

* * * * *

At last another teacher has been found. He is from Madras, and is actually willing to come to distant Ramidi. In fact he has come! A post card from the circle catechist announced his arrival. Now to leave everything standing, lying, falling, as it pleases, and fly to Ramidi and start the school!

Two days later. I found the teacher and his nice little wife established in the house; a rather fine house, with a large front-room big enough for about fifty pupils, and living-rooms for the teacher behind. Much gratitude is due to the Overseer for having managed this so well. We visited people all the afternoon; officials promised to support the school; families who had girls promised to send them. Everything looked prosperous. For the next day we arranged to have a proclamation with tomtoms throughout the town announcing the opening of the school for girls. I was to come again by the midday train and lend glory to the procession; the new teacher was to be in evidence, and Ezekiel the catechist, who was visibly swelling with pride and joy at the prospect, was to read the proclamation. I returned home by the night train and was back at Ramidi next midday. The train was an hour late, but fortunately I had brought the cycle and flew along in great haste, fearing to keep the tomtom men waiting. At the entrance to the town stood Ezekiel alone. I jumped off. "Where are the tomtom men?"

[1] Merchant owning toddy shops.

He gurgled and stuttered, no voice seemed to come; his eyes had grown smaller and sought the ground; his chest, but yesterday so puffed out, had sunk in; his head hung forward in a deprecatory way, he looked like nothing on earth but a collapsing balloon. "Please speak up, Mr. Ezekiel!" I entreated. "What has happened?"

Slowly it came out in depressed stutters. Several people in the town had set to the previous evening after I had left and frightened the house-owner.

"Why did you give it to Christians? Don't you know they are all low caste? Your house will be defiled if you allow it . . ." working upon his fears and prejudices with such success that late at night he went to the teacher. "You cannot stay here," he announced. "Take your things away. The school must not be kept here. I don't want any rent for these few days. Only go. This time to-morrow the house must be empty."

"And so," added Ezekiel with a funereal air, "I did not bring the tomtom men."

I felt sick all down my spine. Also, for the moment, quite horribly lonely. If the Overseer had still been here it would not have happened, I thought disconsolately. But he was gone. No helper in sight. Ezekiel was no use, though a kindly and good man; but he has no stamina or initiative. Nothing but hostile forces around. To crown all, in the train journey a fit of internal pains had come on, and I had to exert all my will to keep the disagreeable physical consciousness in the background. A crowd was gathering round us, staring at two disheartened people and the wholly unhelpful bicycle.

"Let us move on at all events," I said, "and get the owner and speak to him."

We walked to the school where the teacher and his wife sat in depression among their belongings, wishing themselves well away in their own friendly native place.

The owner arrived, looking hard and stern. On him was concentrated all the persuasiveness that could be scraped up anywhere within. With great candour I repeated for him all the objections that I had heard had been raised. The man nodded their truth in acknowledgment; I made sympathetic noises in return. I allowed the objections to be weighty. His severe aspect relaxed a little, seeing I so fully grasped his difficulties. Evidently, he began to think, I was convinced by them; but alack, I turned round and proceeded to demolish them one by one. A little laughter moved into action, a little flavour of wider horizons showed in the rear. Then all artillery was withdrawn, and speech became a frank appeal from one human being to another not to break faith, that in dependence on his word to give the house we had made all arrangements. "Look at the teacher," I wound up, "his wife, his child, his baby; see all their belongings; can they be put into the street? If you do this is it merit to you? Or is it sin?"

"Sin," he acknowledged, hard pressed; and up marched further battalions, amongst them, I am sorry to say, irregulars letting off arrows of flattery. "Enlightened men like you help to bring light to ignorant ones; instead of being influenced by the fearful ones in the town, by those without any sense, it is your part to teach them; if you stand for the cause of education, fame will come to your name . . ." every last and least resource was drummed up.

"You have seen and known many things," the man acknowledged; "we only know this town."

The hostile ranks are wavering, I thought joyfully, but at that moment an uncle and other relatives came in, bringing up reserves.

"This is my elder and superior," the house-owner said. "Talk to him. All our family listen to his words," and beat a retreat himself. Oh Indian love of shifting responsibility!

So it had to be done all over again. In the new-comer I recognized a straightforward spirit and pursued all the more my tactics of taking for granted that we were friends and that he desired every one's best; I spoke frankly of our embarrassment if they turned us out, and appealed to his chivalry.

"We are thinking of the teacher," the opponent declared, shifting his ground. "It may be hard for them in this town."

"That is our look out," I said valiantly. "If he dies of any disagreeables here I will bear you witness that you warned us and that it is not your fault. It is very kind of you to be concerned for him. If you would appoint a coolie to bring him water he will manage nicely. If you will allow us to make a beginning here, we could look round for another house to move the school to presently."

That suggestion of compromise caught him at last.

"Very well, begin here." With a friendly salaam he withdrew. There was no time for more than one sigh of thankfulness. Over two hours had gone.

"Mr. Ezekiel! Can we get the tomtom men now?"

"I will get them," he said, and disappeared. During the battle I had watched his eyes grow larger, his chest expand, his head become erect; visibly he swelled, until the whole balloon was complete again and in the best of condition to spout the proclamation throughout the highways and byways of Ramidi.

* * * * *

Next day I woke with an extraordinary sense of buoyancy; many waters could not drown it, neither physical *malaise* (which still plagued), nor fatigue, nor hardship, nor any other thing. Is it others' prayer? It is as if great streams of spiritual vitality were flowing into one's being. Whatever the cause, God be thanked for it. To be walking a path beset with difficulties, companioned by a lovely sense of unconquerableness, is a treasure not to be exchanged for all the kingdoms of the world and the glory of them. Perhaps one has to come to out-of-the-way corners of the earth, where ventures of faith await one, to find it.

* * * * *

Evening. Perhaps it was a kindly provision from the Unseen to fortify one against a coming need. For uphill the way remains. Early this morning I was off to the town, having slept in the tiny tent which Suleiman could manage to pitch under the banyan-tree by the river. My heart beat high with excitement. How was the school starting? Should I find a gay crowd? Ten children—twenty?

But silence and emptiness greeted me instead. The teacher's wife came from an inner room and explained that two children had come and seeing no one else ran away again in a fright. The schoolmaster was out now searching for children. Some people had said that to-day being full moon was not an auspicious day, they would send girls in a few days. A Mahratta family wanted me to go round to their house now and hear what they had to say.

I went and learned that the town was terrified of a Christian teacher. It is Venkata Raju who is the secret enemy; it was he who disturbed the house-owner's mind and nearly succeeded in ejecting us, and who was now sowing seeds of distrust and fear all over the town where in the general ignorance and prejudice they find a ready soil. How will a school be possible with no local support and constant secret opposition? But when I began to wonder if after all failure was to be my lot the people of the house turned round and became encouragers.

"Don't think your school won't succeed; don't close it in a hurry; it will come, go patiently for a little. In a few days our daughter returns from a visit, she shall come and the little sister with her."

Much cheered, I thanked them and left the house to walk round the town again and talk to parents. In the end I arrived at the school with five or six girls; presently these swelled to eight and with these we started. This beginning will have to be carefully nursed; it is a much more difficult beginning than I thought; but I am prepared to exert any amount of patience.

Next day. Well, I don't know. I rather wish I need not. The stock of hope threatens to run out. I found the girls are not Ramidi girls at all, but visitors who will go away again. The teacher, however, came with three little new Brahmin pupils who are residents. Girls in Venkata Raju's school say they will come in a few days, after the inspection.

> "And does the road lead uphill all the way?
> Yes, to the very end."

Though I remain bent on climbing I have certainly begun to pant and puff a little and to find the path steep.

CHAPTER X

THE path remains steep.

I am writing from Ootacamund, where I have waked in the glorious dawn among the Blue Mountains. The birds are singing in uncontrollable ecstasy; the grass is almost white with dew except where the sun has kissed it; the daisies are delicately nodding on slender stems in a scarcely perceptible breeze. Beyond the lawn stands a tall, deep fir, a whole world of mystery between its branches, to the inner depths of which no one can penetrate, not even the sunshine; no dew sparkles there, life's gaiety seems far from it. Like an incarnation of Solemnity it stands there, suggesting the presence of grave problems in the midst of a sparkling, singing, smiling world, yet itself perhaps the most beautiful thing in it.

Into the midst of this morning happiness came the post. A letter from the Ramidi teacher, but not with the Ramidi postmark. With fear and trembling I opened it and felt sick and sicker as I read it. He wrote that he had fallen ill and could not bear the troubles in that place any longer; if he stayed he would surely have died. So he had gone to his own village near Madras, after leaving the school in the charge of the head constable. A letter from Ezekiel by the same post said he left it to Venkata Raju; before the head constable he arranged with that arch enemy that *he* should teach our school and receive a salary. He had locked up our school building and the girls were now being taught in Venkata Raju's school.

The whole laboriously erected building toppled down at one stroke! And here I am four hundred miles or so distant from the scene of action. I want to fly down, but common sense forbids it in the midst of the hot weather; I could not return all this way, and a holiday is a simple and sheer necessity. What to do then? In my brain, benumbed with dismay, a sentence in Ezekiel's letter about his daughter being with them on a visit began to stand out. She is a trained teacher. That is the way of escape! Off to the telegraph office; urgent wires sped away with injunctions and requests. Instead of a walk in the heavenly morning further letters had to be written to every one concerned.

* * * * *

Now it is evening. What are the puny events of the day? I have been looking at the miracles of God among the hills. On Sunset Hill I gazed on one side over the sea of downs, soft grass-clad hills like green waves suddenly solidified; on the other side valleys of thick jungle opened out, leading to great ranges in the distance; behind me stood the near and wooded hills rising directly over Ooty itself. Every way one looked was so distracting with beauty that one envied the apocalyptic animals with their eyes behind and before. The sun was out, but the sky full of clouds travelling across the sun in all directions, throwing part of the landscape into shadow, irradiating the rest with brilliant patches of sunshine. The rapidity of the change bewildered me; now this peak flashed out, now that; features on distant hills never seen before stood suddenly clearly illuminated, framed by shadow; then faded into greyness again. The shining came closer; the near downsland suddenly stood forth in inexpressible glory, every motherly curve and hollow of the hillsides was picked out till one could almost distinguish the separate grass blades. It passed backwards, and the distant ranges shone as the streets of gold. A streak of meadowland by a far-off wood flashed out like a twinkling smile dawning in the eye of the landscape; it broadened till the whole hillside was bathed in laughter; still travelling on, the very mountains were moved to gaiety; it was as if a huge assembly had been affected by the merriment of an individual and now shared the mirth. Still from second to second its mood altered. There was no time to take in a perfect picture before another perfect one hung in its place. I gasped at the wasteful splendour!

The downs tempted me farther afield to the hill we have named "Eureka." Thence, if you are lucky, as I sometimes have been, you may see the little hills dancing together. But to-night they were far from dancing, they were too frightened. For by the time we reached there things had greatly changed. Ooty and its woods and hills indeed still lay in the sunshine, a clear blue sky hung serenely over it, but towards the west the clouds had piled up a black menace that was moving towards us, devouring all reassurance out of the sky till it towered overhead like an embodiment of threatening Fate; one depth of blackness after another reinforced it from the horizon where the very powers of the Inferno were balling themselves together in midnight gloom. Still the sinister tiers came steadily moving towards us, always revealing still greater masses of storm behind, making one's heart beat wildly at the beauty and the awe of forces so enormous, so careless of our puniness; menacing, it would seem, all peace and serenity in the universe, yet marching to the rhythm of some majestic law.

On it came, this vast army of destruction; the wind flew dank and chill before it; the light mists leapt down from distant boulders and ran for the valleys; I also turned to flee before the resistless advance of the storm and, turning, saw Ooty lying clear and smiling in the sunshine, untroubled by the woe and wildness in the west. With a roar as of the trump of doom the storm broke long before we had covered the four miles home; no matter, the picture of that radiant peace, serene and steadfast while the hosts of darkness marched in upon it remains an unforgotten spot of glory in my memory.

Whatever it means it can mean no less than that the Power

that is behind that conquering darkness and yet unconquered light is not beyond dealing with affairs in Ramidi!

* * * * *

Later. Holidays are over. Help came in Ramidi. Ezekiel's daughter Salome cast in her lot with us and is working up the school splendidly. There are thirty-two girls and I hope the venture is now afloat for good. Meanwhile fresh efforts are being made to gain an opening for the boys. But Naraina is vacillating and Venkatu Raju works against us all the time. Patience and still more patience is required in the East!

Bukkuru. I bless Brierley for the many helps he gives; his words have often been like sentinels guarding the avenues along which resentment, discouragement and the fatal sense of futility of all effort assault the soul. "Our life is . . . a continuous extraction from the raw material of circumstance, of certain inner states." "Shall we grumble at a world whose worst assaults are, after all, opportunities for winning inner victories?" These sentences have been my inspiration this week, which has been a rather terrible one. I felt as if life had me by the hair, but, helped by those words, I had it by the throat.

News of further trouble at Bukkuru brought me here. The train leaves at 6 a.m. I had my Hindustani Testament with me and was soon entranced. In a fresh language the familiar story becomes entirely new. I read, slowly unravelling the sense, that He climbed a hill and sat there, and that they brought to Him a great crowd of deaf and lame and blind and He healed them all (Matt. xv. 29). The passage, in Hindustani, was quite unexpected and made a vivid picture of that gracious, beset Figure, surrounded by this crowd of deformities. Are not physical deficiencies apt to be repelling? And He, with His perfect sense of beauty, did He never feel tempted to shrink from those human uglinesses? Pressed upon by them, assaulted probably by the whining tone of the Eastern suppliant, He never flinched. "He—healed them." Each deformity was an appeal. While we, when we have to do with spiritually blind and lame, with people who have no self-knowledge, or backbone, or perseverance, are repelled almost immediately.

In spite of the fortification of this meditation I sighed soon afterwards. The cart ride after the train journey seemed endless; headachy and hungry I arrived at noon. The little rest-house was not swept out, nor water ready. Radha stood there and burst into tears when she greeted me; her rheumatic knee had given way and caused a fall in which her cheek had been hurt. "My eye might have been put out," she wept.

Brave, bright Radha, fighting her fight courageously, yet under the feminine necessity of leaning on someone sometimes. "When you come I feel like crying," she said artlessly. I understood well enough her desire to let go occasionally. I should like it myself! At this very moment, for instance. After a night of little sleep and a tiring journey, and the servant announcing he had forgotten the food basket, I unfeignedly yearn to cease from strenuousness, but it is the auspicious moment chosen by Radha to have **her** cry out. At length she wiped her tears and said without further preamble, "Marala Subbamma is dead."

"What? *What* are you saying? Marala Subbamma is dead?"

"Yes, she died of fever. News came two weeks ago."

Hunger and headache were forgotten now. The news stunned me: my poor little Brahmin widow! I am certain that she was neglected and need not have died. No one wanted her to live; perhaps she did not want to herself. It is grievous to think that probably no one wept for her but her Christian friends. I have sent for Prema to tell me some further details.

Poor lazy little Subbamma, with her longing for happiness and her fitful efforts. "When you are here and talk to me," she said last time, "I want to do everything, I want to be a Christian, I want to pray, I want to learn and be educated; but you go away again; it is difficult alone, no one cares and then in the end I don't care either."

J'accuse! I want to say to India and its treatment of young widows.

The post arrived and hurled a bolt from the blue. A Taluk Board Girls' School is to be opened in Ramidi on Saturday (to-morrow); on this account recognition is refused to the Mission school.

I am thunderstruck. All had been going well there: the Inspectress was in favour of recognizing it. What can have caused this new departure? But I have no intention of letting Ramidi girls' school go again. On my last visit I found the little scholars improving in moral feeling. The teacher on re-entering had asked "Who has been out while I was away?"

"Not I! not I! not I!" cried everybody. But two or three had been, and *the whole school* turned on them: "Are you not afraid? Has not God seen you?"

The development of a conscience in Ramidi I hope will be continued. But if the Taluk Board opens a girls' school there will be no room for a Mission school, it would be good-bye to Christian influence in the town. In this the Board have acted against rules, as already a school is in existence, and rivalry is not permitted. I am losing no time in protesting by letter and telegram. But "to-morrow" it is to be opened! For this once I am praying the East to procrastinate as usual.

The Ramidi news was not the only letter. Andapur school is also in the wars now. The headmaster of the Government Girls' School has been busy sheep-stealing; my capable Balamma writes a long screed of utter discouragement. The school is being called the *Mala* and *Madiga* (i.e. low caste) school; four more girls have been taken; others are following; the children are in confusion; they themselves want to come;

but the parents, influenced by the hostile headmaster, prevent them. Balamma adds that she cannot bear all this trouble; she has had enough of it. I rather want to say that myself.

Meanwhile some Mohammedans arrived with their tale of woe about the disturbance here. The cause is the quarrelling of the Mohammedans among themselves and the teacher's husband having joined one faction. The other factions now, with curious Eastern logic, try to ruin his wife's school. They are a very implacable set of people here; in all other places one sacred Wall where prayer is performed suffices for the whole community; but here, during one of these disagreements, they had to build a second one for the newest intolerants.

Later on I went to examine the school. The Christian teacher's work could be commended; but she has only sewing, arithmetic, drill; reading and writing, taught by the Mohammedan teacher, was certainly not good. This is what happened this morning:—

I. "Put down your slates. Now spell '*bāp*.'" The children gazed at me in silence.

I. "What letters should you write to make '*bāp*'?"

A bright pupil. "B—p."

I. "That makes '*bap*.'" Before I have time to add, "But I want you to spell '*bāp*,'" they were after me like nimble parrots. "That makes '*bâp*'." [1]

"Listen, children. I want you to spell '*bāp*.'"

"*b*, *b*," they began again hesitatingly, half of them by this time not attending as there was nothing to repeat apparently.

"All of you look here. *b* always makes *bâ*—what have you to add——"

But I did not get it out. Having heard something familiar a joyful chorus immediately interrupted, "*b* always makes *bâ*." A few longer-eared ones added, "What have you to add to make it *bā*?"

[1] The difference in a long and short vowel.

One can see what they are accustomed to. Yet they are not at all devoid of intelligence. I left the reading and tried them with stories and drawing. The request to the teacher to tell them an easy story drew a blank, so I launched my frail bark of Hindustani on the story of the merchant seeking goodly pearls.

"Now draw it, children."

The pearls were managed creditably, also striking anatomies representing the merchant, replete in spite of his exertions, or else worn sadly out of shape by them. One little genius had introduced a doubtful creation, explained to be a cow.

"What is that cow for?"

"That's the cow he sold to get the money for the pearl." Top marks!

After a further interview the Mohammedans agreed to forgo quarrels and support the school. The teacher and her husband, having it impressed upon them that the school stood for peace and righteousness, promised every sort of amends. It would be well to stay here for a while and help them steer steadily for these ideals, but now there is further news of trouble in Dharmpalli, making it imperative to go there at once. Ramidi and Andapur are also urgently calling. The delivery of the post causes palpitations nowadays; nothing but news of disasters seems to arrive.

Dharmpalli. The new headmaster of our nice girls' school here declared he must leave at once. His wife is ill, of hysteria, I gather. I told him he must give me time to make fresh arrangements, but what arrangements to make I do not know. I shall have to know quite soon; for it is no use keeping a man bent on going. Poor fellow, he came in great distress to show where his wife had bitten his arm; domestically all is shadow for him; the school is naturally affected by the gloom.

Andapur. When I arrived here I found another cheerless post awaiting me. Salome, the great mainstay of our Ramidi school, wrote that she wants to go back to her former post. Between her leaving and the new Board School, Ramidi school is certainly doomed. And here is Balamma with a depressed countenance saying things in Andapur are no better but rather worse. " The world is out of joint."

Next day. The post continues its habit of dealing blows. This morning I was greeted by a note from the Dharmpalli catechist; the teacher (who, I had fondly hoped, had been persuaded to stay and hold the fort a little longer) had left, and who was to take charge of the school ?

I wish I knew! But now the worm is turning. The unkind fates are piling it on too much. If two or three things go wrong and mean to discourage me, all right, I'll be discouraged. But when every mortal thing that can go wrong does go wrong I will not oblige any longer!

Into the middle of utmost perplexity, when Dharmpalli was tottering, Andapur weakening, Bukkuru unsafe, Ramidi, apparently, already fallen, flashed the thought, " Our *faith* is the victory "—thank God, not our success.

" Life is a continuous extraction from the raw material of circumstance of certain inner states." Raw indeed is my material, but with it comes the chance of working at the artistry of life. " Shall we grumble at a world whose worst assaults are, after all, opportunities for winning inner victories ? " Having won those the resolution to win outward ones also seems to follow as a matter of course.

I went to the Andapur school. From Balamma's wails I had expected an almost empty school; but there were twenty-nine children. Of course it is not good—still it seemed to me the hostile forces were wavering just a little before a resolute inner front, stayed upon nothing tangible.

On the way back the telegraph *peon* handed me a wire. It was from Mr. Maitland, the friend and fellow-missionary to whom I had written for advice about Ramidi. " Ramidi project outrageous. See Collector. Board cannot enter into rivalry. One school sufficient," ran the friendly and inspiring message, taking away the always threatening sense of loneliness and pointing the direction of fresh effort.

No time was lost in following it.

It turned out that our new Collector was himself responsible for the Ramidi project.

" I did not know you had started a school there," said the friendly official. " I will go and see it. If I like it I will stop this one."

" Thank you very much. When ? "

" On Tuesday morning."

It does not give us much time. The great thing is to get Salome to put her heart into Ramidi. A special messenger left with a letter for her and her father, advising her of the Collector's coming.

Next day. It was as well I used the next train and did not wait for the post which goes at night; for Salome meanwhile had posted her actual resignation which arrived this morning. The post, you perceive, keeps on with its antics, and the hostile forces are evidently making a stand. But I continue in a victorious mood. Hard upon the post came the return messenger with a letter from Ezekiel saying he had succeeded in persuading Salome to withdraw her resignation. She would do her best to have a good school on next Tuesday. What Salome puts her back into will be a success, and I can go now with an easier mind (to speak in a human manner) to Dharmpalli to see what local help I can raise to keep that school afloat.

A week later. Arriving back here late last night from Dharmpalli, I found a telegram waiting. The post having been so unkind of late, I cannot get rid of a little nervousness and fear of bad news. But this is what it was: " No Board School to be opened Ramidi for the present. Taluk Board and District Board Presidents both recommend aiding your school. Collector."

" Thank God," I said with a little tear of gladness, and then jubilantly danced round the dining-table. The last and most dangerous rock passed in safety and Ramidi ship out in the open sailing! That school has been nearly killed so many times that I can scarcely believe it is a strapping infant at last. (Never mind mixed metaphors.) It was nearly stillborn when the owner refused the house, then what a puny, feeble babe for three months! Not till April did it show any signs of life. The teacher bolting in May was again almost fatal to it. Salome's coming revived it, but the imminent Board School laid throttling hands on it. Then I yelled for dear life, and the Collector came like a giant Greatheart and saved it. He did more than he was asked; not only stopped the rival school but recommended ours for aid at the various Boards. *Jayam, jayam,*[1] hallelujah!

Andapur, months later. At long last another goal has been reached. Naraina, after endless hesitations has transferred his school to the Mission. A Christian headmaster was also found—miracles do not cease! It is true when he arrived at Ramidi and saw what kind of place it was, its drunkenness, its quarrels, its immorality, his spirit was sickened. "I thought I had come to the mouth of hell," he wrote. But he faced it bravely. He is so efficient a man that very soon boys began to leave other schools and crowd to ours. English, well taught, is a great attraction. We started with thirty boys, and we have nearly a hundred now!

I have been to the first sports prize-giving at Ramidi. Wind and dust storms are at present the order of the day; it thunders, the sky is black; then comes a terrific hurricane; I begin to tremble lest the house should not stand it; that at least all the tiles will be blown off. (Some have.) I run and shut every door and window; if not, everything movable goes over: papers, photos, flowers, rugs, all things begin to dance, or fly, or fall, or bang, according to their nature; standing-lamps have crashed; pictures torn themselves loose, the whirlwind spares nothing. It came on like that at our Ramidi prize-giving. We were almost blinded with sand

[1] Victory.

and dust—all the sand in the river seemed to rise upon us. What cared I? We held the function in the market halls where I had stood one rainy day and felt forlorn. To-day again the hall was full from end to end, but this time they were all our boys. I looked down the long rows of faces, eager and smiling in spite of the grit and dust covering us all, and sang the Doxology in my heart.

More than ever do I believe in what I call my thought-pocket. That is a magical receptacle! Stuff an idea into it, keep it there, never let it go, and some time out comes a new and miraculous fact—a materialized phenomenon. Thoughts are *things*!

At Ramidi station nowadays there are no more rude cart drivers. Smiling, deferential schoolboys fly to render every possible service. Our headmaster was chosen as a member of the Union. The well which worried me on my first visit has been enclosed. The toddy shop is outside the town now. Sanitary regulations are enforced.

In the houses my dear Lois is doing a splendid work. I saw a woman who has learned from A B C upwards with her, and now reads the Gospel fluently. In Ramidi!

There are five or six more women pupils in that place; formerly so frightened of women learning to read.

Now I have rammed buildings of our own, for the boys' school, and the girls' school, for the workers living here, into that capacious thought-pocket—and in a little corner of it snuggles securely, safe against being let out, a Christian Church.

As I stood in the market hall and saw that from having no place or influence we were coming to a stage where practically the whole education of the town is passing into Christian hands, imagination ran riot. I can now conceive of a faith that can subdue kingdoms, turn to flight armies—work any miracle. If only we were not such fools and blind and slow of heart to believe—why, we could move the universe!

When we all, the earth, all peoples and all races, have learned to do the will of God as it is done in Heaven, we *shall*.

CHAPTER XI

THE monsoon winds are howling and tearing over the plains; they rave like lost spirits, mad for some relief and finding none. Everything is covered with dust; doors bang unless well fastened back; mats fly up; pictures knock against the walls; the canvas in the verandah chairs flops up and down; the *tatties* [1] scrape against the pillars: everything is restless and nerve racking. And withal it is hot; clouds pile up, but no rain comes.

In this already trying season a fresh set of trials is let loose in my world. For many months now the necessity of a new bungalow has sat like a nightmare upon me. In between the claims of villages and schools Andapur had been tramped over in the search for sites; a suitable one had at length been fixed on and approved by Committee. A well was dug and an enclosing hedge planted; for many days watching it coming into being was a good excuse for an evening walk—walks being of the nature of luxuries nowadays. The trouble then began of interviewing contractors; all demanded higher rates than the estimates allowed, and perplexities grew apace. At length a young *maistry*,[2] trained to some extent in building work by one of our missionaries in Mysore, was recommended to me. He has now come and building operations are beginning. There is no contract; we are to buy our materials as we go along, and employ our own workmen. In spare moments (save the mark!) I pore over building books, and enter a hitherto closed realm of knowledge.

We have got as far as the foundation trenches; now the concrete is to go in. I had been informed that the *maistry* "needed watching"; my heart sank, for what do I know?

[1] Bamboo blinds. [2] Foreman.

Ignorance being complete, however, I care not how much I exhibit it; letters of inquiry and thirst for details go to knowledgeable ones amongst our missionaries who are very kind in responding: thus armed I arrive at the scene of action and strut as an expert.

To-day I observed the many claims the poor *maistry* has to meet. The coolies are mostly so lazy and stupid that every one ought to be watched the whole time. *Chunam,* (lime) which has to be mixed with sand, was being ground in a circular trench by two bulls harnessed to a solid stone wheel: each time the wheel passes over this it ought to be mixed afresh, but the women supposed to be following the wheel and shovelling dawdled, so that the mortar was inadequately ground. Ballast and mortar were to be mixed on a brick floor; but men supposed to be doing it rested on their shovels. Coolies carried the mixed stuff in baskets to the trenches; but they got in each other's way and then stood still; the men in the trenches poured in the concrete anyhow, careless about maintaining a level; the workman tamping it would not lift his arm properly, the tamper being heavy; yet unless it comes down with force the concrete will not be properly rammed. The coolies sent for water lounged about at the well—all of them want perpetually to go away for this and that—it was exasperating, however much one may preach to oneself that one cannot hurry the East.

* * * * *

Feeling nervous about the concrete work not being right I had asked Mr. Arling if he could come in and see it; he came and found it wrong. The mortar, he declared, was not mixed rightly and would not set hard, he said; the ramming was not good; the sand stored was either too fine or too coarse, but never just right: my heart went down and down, and so did the *maistry's.* The one encouraging thing was the excellence of the soil which apparently will neutralize the bad concrete. Why then did we dig trenches? But having dug them we must now fill them up. The well, recently deepened, threatened to give out again. After we had left the site came an urgent message that it was completely exhausted; would I please see that the municipal water-cart was sent at once? I did so. In the afternoon I went over to see that all the suggested improvements were carried out. A commotion was going on; I learned that the shaft of the municipal water-cart had broken.

The poor *maistry* turned quite faint at this last blow; Mr. Arling's criticisms, the well drying up, and now the cart smashing when we needed floods of water for the concrete work, seemed to immerse us all in the Slough of Despond. This building work makes me feel I shall drown in it quite frequently. It is positively worse than schools.

A man who had climbed down the well reported that the rock at the bottom was not non-porous white granite, which is very hard to blast, but some other kind of rock which can be tackled. Wherefore it is going to be tackled, also the blacksmith is to come and patch up the rotten shaft which, I was told, had been risky before. My waterman, Nursana, who is worth five coolies, has tied it up, so to speak, with rope, and it is holding together, as it were. So we fight our way. Then the *maistry* announced the ballast was coming to an end, also the lime; it was necessary for him to go to a village three miles away and get more, would I please take charge in the morning.

* * * * *

I did, and it was a case of "the Aryan smiles and the Christian riles" all the time. I was there before seven o'clock; only half the coolies had come. Concrete was brought to the mixing floor and coolies set sifting sand; then the oxen arrived for grinding it. As soon as they are on the spot their driver wants the grinding channel filled with the stuff, for he is paid for each lot he completes. I ran to see if there were enough sifted lime—yes, for one lot, but not the next—so hey presto! we must slake more lime; " bring water to slake the burnt lime!" Meanwhile the mixture going in had to be counted; fifty baskets of sand, twenty-five of lime—in, in, now bring water for mixing—" Here, oh coolie, don't scrape the top, mix it properly from the bottom!"

" Ho, ho, you ballast-bringing people, why are you standing still ? "

Off I ran to that floor. " Pour it evenly! Nine inches high—take your measure stick and see. Lingappa, you have sense, see that it is done right. Now water, bring water, water! the stones must be wetted before pouring the mortar on! There, measure please, three inches high only for the mortar."

" Oh, trench coolies! Can you not see the concrete is getting dry ? Pour water as long as it will soak in."

Back to my future kitchen where the lime was being slaked; an infernal heat filled it, water on the quicklime giving off enormous heat and steam. " Modeen Bi, keep on sifting more lime; it is wanted for the next grinding," and so on *ad infinitum.*

I would not be a *maistry* for anything. It might be enjoyable to keep one's mind on half a dozen occupations and calculate what is wanted for each, in advance; but the execution! through brains of an unbelievable slowness. " Don't bring any more sand; go for lime now." " It is enough, put down your basket and help at the well." " Lay the concrete in *this* place. Do *look* where I am showing you!" etc.

Meanwhile the carpenters arrived. " What shall we saw? "

I declined to give them instructions, knowing they had already received them from the *maistry*, and that this question was only a labour-saving device.

" The water-cart is smashed again," a voice broke in

upon my indignant meditation over the carpenters, deflecting it into a, by now, familiar channel.

Put not thy trust in blacksmiths. India, certainly, generally prefers string. So shall we. Great is the force of example!

"Nursana, will you do the rope trick once more?"

Nursana obliges. The cart holds together again in a fragile manner.

"The coolie has let the rope and pot fall into the well."

"Lingappa! Climb down the well and get it up again."

Will it go on like this? "You have not begun yet," said Mr. Arling yesterday. In that case, though the bungalow is not likely to be finished, I shall be. And then

> Under this wide and windy sky
> Dig my grave and let me lie.
> And this is the script ye shall grave for me:
> "Of building a bungalow here died she!"
>
> (With apologies to R.L.S.)

Picture it all in a temperature of about 200°, I should say, for there is not an atom of shade; not a tree, not a bush—what a job it will be to make a garden near the house! Aha, then after all do I expect it to be finished before I am?

Returning home tired and tending to be ruffled, a line came into my mind, like cleansing sea water on a dust-covered body. I could remember no context, just this:

> "With a secret purpose of glory in every part."

I bless the poet whoever he or she is. For what more is wanted to help one over such hours? The doors of the universe swing back; one finds oneself linked to everything great and everlasting. Can there be a secret purpose of glory in bricks and ballast or broken water-carts? Yes, the influence for God and good that shall emanate from this house when it is finished, down the vista of the years. Yes, the Future, when others will be here (who will be saved this struggle of building anyhow), when we shall have . . . here the purpose merges into dreams. Dreams for the moment have a tendency towards bricks and mortar. Not only a bungalow for the women missionaries, I see in anticipation a good building for the Mohammedan school, also one for the Hindu school; and if that Andapur Town Extension beyond the railway comes to anything, a good school and building there; above all a Home for girls and women where there is now a wilderness; also a building of our own in Ramidi—oh yes, and a boys' school there and a building for *that*, and a building in Dharmpalli—what good things we are making for by urging on the coolies to sift sand and tamp concrete! Joyfully I hitch my wagon to these stars and with an eye raised to them steadfastly crack my common whip.

* * * * *

In between building operations and their tendency to harness the mind to outward details and harassing difficulties, uplifting events may happen. I had to go to Bukkuru on a flying visit and while there received a call from Lachmi Nursana, a Brahmin *purohit*,[1] one of India's choice spirits. In his town, two miles from Bukkuru, he does things very unusual for a Brahmin priest. He cares for the outcastes. Their quarters were dirty and ill-lit; on the council of the Union he advocated that they, as well as the caste people, should have street lanterns. The other members were unwilling to spend a penny of town money on outcastes, but he fought it through. He also started a night school for young men, himself paying the teacher. Outcastes wanted to come to it. He allowed them. Then the teacher, a Brahmin, objected. When Lachmi Nursana insisted, the teacher left. Undaunted, he taught the school himself. After six weeks of steady perseverance another teacher was found, and this reformer had carried the day. The outcastes still come.

To-day he told me he was first stirred up to help others

[1] Household priest.

and teach the ignorant by reading a gospel of John. It made him want to read the whole Bible.

"But I don't understand it all yet," he confessed. We had a talk on the way in which it had been built up through centuries. It was truly heart warming to hear this man's reverence and love for Jesus Christ.

"If only all understood," he added. "There are foolish prejudices. I was reading about Him one day and friends came in. 'What are you reading?' they asked. 'The Bible,' I replied. 'The Christians' book!' '*Chi, chi*,'[1] they said, spat on the ground and left the house.

"Some time after it happened again that I was reading the life of Christ when they came in. They asked what I was reading this time.

"'A book written by a man called Luke,' I answered.

"'We never heard of him,' they said. 'Read what he says.' So I read.

"'What beautiful words,' they remarked, 'very beautiful words. Who is this writer?'

"I explained he was a Christian and this was part of the Bible. They begged my pardon for having been so rude before. 'You must excuse us, sir; we did not know the Bible was such a beautiful book. Will you please read it to us again?'"

Other encouraging things also I learned to-day from my friend. As *Purohit* he has access to homes and gets to know some of the inner things there. "Many of your old schoolgirls in Bukkuru read the Bible," he said, "secretly, because their husbands are averse to it. Here also in Patacheruvu I know of at least one who reads it. I encourage them in it."

What pictures this conjured up! The Brahmin priest, in the privacy of Hindu homes, advising women to go on reading of Christ. How many schools ought we not to have,

[1] An expression of contempt and disgust.

for boys and girls, to start them in the practice, and make it an intelligible and profitable one?

I was to learn more of such things soon. For I am finishing this in Penuroy where I have come to see Mr. Rangavachari for a special purpose. This is no less than to ask him to put into simple Telugu some parables and Gospel stories re-written for the villages. These, I hope, may be printed as leaflets, comprehensible to those village boys who can read and who embarrass me by requests for something to read. For what can a villager, boy or adult, make of even a gospel? Proper names are puzzling; other terms, Pharisees, synagogue, etc., complete the bewilderment. Let us get into their mental shoes and read the first few verses of any of the four. Even Mark the simple confronts him with John, Jerusalem, Judæa, Jordan at once, and shocks the Indian vegetarian with food of locusts, and perplexes him with a rite called baptism.

Mr. Rangavachari was waiting for me at the Rest-House when I arrived somewhat dishevelled after eighteen miles in the cart. That man has the quickest, courtliest understanding. "You are tired from the journey; you will want a bath. I will just wait here; I have nothing to do. Take an hour, or as long as you like." He had come at *my* request, not on his business at all, and is a busy lawyer! I performed a hurried toilet, then we talked on end. He is going to translate the stories. Is it not good of him? He liked the diamond story and the market story; I could see he was less enthusiastic about the story of Zaccheus and the others, but he will do them nevertheless. He told me one of their stories in return. A disciple of Krishna was so devoted that the god appeared to him and offered to bestow any gift he chose. The man said, "To serve at thy feet—to have fellowship with all thy worshippers, to love all living things—that is my choice."

"And what could be more beautiful," added Rangavachari, "than this answer?"

"Only this," I said, "and is it not the crowning feature of Christianity? *And to save someone lost.* That is what the story of Zaccheus illustrates; he was being lost."

"Let us make him a toddy-shop keeper in the story," suggested Rangavachari, "a toll-gate keeper is not known to untravelled villagers, nor is he despised."

Well, why not?

Is it not a fine step forward to be able to say "we"? So slow and imperceptible is our advance, that sometimes it is only by pulling up sharp and looking back that we see how far we have travelled. How much must the atmosphere in India have been affected by Christ that now a Christian missionary and a Hindu lawyer can put their heads together and produce leaflets which the missionary considers suitable for distribution and which the Hindu admits to be helpful!

Erana brought my tea; Rangavachari offered to go away if I liked; I invited him to stay if *he* did not mind. Inquiring the nature of the meal he asked permission to share it. A doer of his words and not a talker only is this Hindu. "I wish you had time to stay and meet my friend," he said. "He is the Registrar here, a very orthodox Brahmin. He is also a diligent reader of the Bible in private. One day when I was worried and depressed he came in; and seeing me thus what do you think he said?"

"What?" I asked with curiosity. For the comfort one man gives to another in trouble is always a matter of deep interest.

"He said, 'Why do you not tell Jesus? I always do. I find He helps me.'"

"I hope you followed the advice," I replied. Visions arose in my mind of the interior of strict Brahmin houses where prayer was offered to Jesus Christ, where witness was borne to Him between non-Christian friends, where He was found to be a very present help in time of trouble.

Missionaries in India seem to be building better than they know.

CHAPTER XII

THERE is a tide in the affairs of schools which, taken at the flood, leads on to fortune. Such a tide has set in, at last, in Bukkuru. Giriappa wrote that Sita Ramana's school has practically collapsed; he tried again with decent teachers, but as he never paid salaries they always left after brief spells. Now he cannot get anyone; his mistress is doubtless lazy, so no school is held. When any person of importance visits Bukkuru some children are hastily collected and Sita Ramana and his mistress teach them. There is much discontented talk in the town now. I am waiting for them to say definitely "We want the Mission to have the school back again."

That dreamed-of event is lifting a smiling face over the horizon. The Inspectress is helping by surprise visits. On the first occasion she travelled by day; her servant with the official badge was recognized, the tidings of her imminent arrival outran her. Sita Ramana in hot haste collected pupils, and when the Inspectress came a school was in being, and sworn to have been in being every day. But when questioned the teacher could not say for certain *when* he had come; first it was July, then May, when pressed again a wavering June was mentioned. Sita Ramana, who had marked him "present" since May, had omitted to prompt him properly. Registers also showed signs of having been written up hastily; festival days were all marked as full school days. A severe warning followed and the threat of withdrawal of aid.

The next time she travelled by night and arrived before anyone was about. The servant was not allowed to go into the town; at eight o'clock the Inspectress stood by the closed school door and waited. Neither teacher nor children appeared. At length Sita Ramana, informed of the waiting officer, came running.

"It has happened only this once; the teacher is ill with fever; she cannot rise, therefore there is no school to-day."

The Inspectress turned away and walked back to the little Rest-House. Who should come round the corner, carrying a pot of water, but Sitamma the teacher! Startled by the sudden appearance of her official superior she salaamed hastily and had no time for calculation.

"Oh, good morning Sitamma. You are well?"

"Yes, quite well," was the witless reply. "You are coming to the school?"

"I have already been. There is none. There is no need for me to go again."

All day Sita Ramana besieged her. But the Inspectress was adamant, there were too many witnesses complaining of the bad conduct of the school; recognition was withdrawn. But grant for this year might be paid if he were willing to sign a document that he would officially close his school at the end of the official year. A bird in the hand was certainly a bird in the hand, thought Sita Ramana, and signed. The welcome news of this signature has just reached me.

Bukkuru. The dream of the last two years has been realized at last. Our school is opened again! Twenty-five girls came yesterday and there are more to-day.

It would be difficult to express my thankfulness and joy in going from one school to the other! Where two years ago we had nothing there are now two flourishing schools. The ache I had every time I went past the silent and locked-up building is now turned into the happiness of a merry and noisy welcome. Some of the new pupils paid a visit to the Rest-House and explained for the tenth time that they were going to come to school every day. They liked coming. They were not at all afraid of me. I believed them, seeing they could not be induced to go! When they did it was but to return and bring others, for the joy of some more old Christmas-cards.

In the town I looked up some old friends. In Rama Reddi's house they were full of many troubles on which they professed to want advice. One was the matter of settling a bridegroom for Rukmini. The mother passed the candidates in review. One was too young, "he is very thin, and the girl is fat," one had an uncertain character, one could not read, one was ugly, another suffered from the same complaint, he was "as tall as a house, oh, but ugly, like the pictures in English books—and he walks like that," strutting about in a peacocky way, till my shoulders heaved, though Rukmini was sitting by and I did not want to hurt her feelings in case he should be the selected one. Her mother apparently felt less punctilious and freely condemned them all, because none of them were rich. Only the ugly one, whose brand of hideousness was of the English type, had a little.

Krishna Murti, the *Karnam's* people, always demand a visit, though the young widow cares nothing for our teaching. We were sitting on her verandah when the *dhobi* woman came in, her small daughter climbing up the steps after her. Stumbling, she put out a hand to save herself; the hem of the Brahmin lady's *sari* was hanging over the verandah edge. The baby hand fumbled near it. "Don't touch!" came a terrific yell from inside the house, whence someone had observed the imminent catastrophe. A volley of abuse followed. The little one would have fallen down the stairs backwards with fright, had not the mother quickly clutched her. The Brahmin woman hastily drew away her *sari*.

"What would it matter?" I said. "The girl nearly fell and hurt herself. Is it a good thing to frighten a harmless child? Does true religion ever require it?"

"*Our* religion consists in things like these," she said stiffly.

Yes, religion consists for many and many a Hindu woman in things like these. Avoid outward defilement, keep caste, fulfil the ceremonies, respect forms; in these lies salvation.

My thoughts strayed to the hem of another garment, touched by a person afflicted with a sickness counted unclean throughout the East. But it was not scolding that met the poor frightened woman.

His religion consisted in things like those.

* * * * *

Marala. I am returning to Andapur by this route and am now writing under the tamarind trees. A herd of goats is trailing through the grove with two little boys in attendance; one had my milk jug; he milked a few spoonfuls from such goats as the other one could catch and hold; the other goats took to sprinting; the boys with my milk jug flew after them. While I strained eyes wistful for more entertainment the whole caboodle was out of sight over the stony hillocks beyond. But the fates are kind. One of the boys, or a third one, has just come past carrying a little new-born kid. An envelope I had thrown away was lying there; he was on it like a harpy, though still afraid; he dropped his kid, touched the paper gingerly. "You may have it," I said generously. He bolted with his treasure, like a crow with a bit of food. True to the simile, out of nowhere more boys collected. Also two women who stared curiously and took an excursion to get round the tent. Another big empty envelope lay on the ground behind; each snatched at it; I could hear them quarrelling as to who should have it. This time I must forgive Erana for not acting according to instructions and burning all old papers! I had no idea they were such treasures. Every old envelope has now been distributed amongst the boys; such magazines as I had with me followed piecemeal. "Not this, I have not read it," I objected to one being seized. "We will wait here till you have read it," they answered with the persevering patience of the East. More boys arrived. "We will *buy* paper, also pens," they announced. Alas! I have no stationer's shop. "Oh, do look well!" they begged disappointedly, eyeing the interior of the tent hopefully. To them, no doubt, it appears a veritable treasure-house. "I have books," I told them. Then began more entertainment. Great sprints were made for home, followed by breathless arrivals, "I have a *bottu*," [1] "I have half an anna," accompanied by wistful looks. "I have one *pie*,"[2]—a more wistful look still. Some plutocrats had a whole anna. My stock of booklets sensibly diminished—so has my time—and here comes Prema.

She brought Pullakka, whom I had not seen since Subbamma's death; she wept according to proper Hindu etiquette. Her conventional grief makes me feel afresh how little poor Subi was cared for and protected here. Was death the only solution for protecting her from the temptations and unhappinesses of the young widow's lot?

Prema had other news. A schoolmaster in a neighbouring village asked her for books. She lent him her book of New Testament stories and showed me what this Hindu had written on the fly-leaf.

"In this book is told how Jesus of the divine nature was born so that He might heal the world. This Great One did many works which were very wonderful. In the end, for the sake of those who believe in Him, He sacrificed even His body. But when this Great One had left the body His story is not finished; for He came again as the Holy Spirit to do more marvellous works and to help those who believe in God."

I looked at the pencil-scrawled lines almost with awe; for they seem to me to indicate a spirit searching after God, and apprehending with great sensitiveness what is divine. Had the writer not grasped the kernel of Christianity?

[1] A quarter of an anna = one farthing. [2] One-twelfth of an anna.

Next day. To-day we went to his village, nestling among the hills; up and down jungly paths we walked, crossing streambeds where bulrushes grew in masses. We at last arrived in a little valley where the brook widened out, great mango trees gave shade, hills enclosed it, after the wide and burning plains it seemed a lovely green spot. The people streamed out of their huts and were pathetically eager and friendly. "No one has ever come to teach us anything." (When I returned to Marala and saw some Brahmins sitting comfortably in the shade doing nothing I passed that remark of the villagers on to them!)

The women were full of the usual questions.

"How many children have you?"

"Hundreds," I replied cheerfully. "You are all my children!"

They nodded and smiled. One poor old woman sat alone on her doorstep. I went over to her. "*Amma*, whom have you with you in the house?"

"No one, no one," she answered, "and who are you? I have lost one eye, now the other is going blind. I can only see you as a dark shape, but I can hear you—how kindly you talk to me!" she burst into tears, poor lonely old soul. "Come and listen, we shall sing now," Prema comforted her. "I will come and visit you again."

The schoolmaster alas! was absent; but we went to his school and collected boys. The crowd surrounded us; the schoolboys read aloud the leaflets we gave them; parents proud of the achievements of their offspring listened willingly to further explanations, and when gospels and booklets were offered for sale we drove a fine trade. The schoolmaster on his return will find copies of the Psalms and the Gospels; may they guide his searching spirit.

A group of coolie women were going out to the fields; as I passed them they stood still in a row to stare. I also stood. "Yes, look. Look as much as you like. Is it a good sight? Do you feel better? Shall I stand still a little longer so that you can look more?" All were laughing by that time, of course.

"Where are you going?" I proceeded.

"To cut *ragi*."

"To cut *ragi*. As you cut will you remember to thank God for giving us the grain?"

"And then our work will be blessed," said a quickly responsive soul amongst them.

"And then your work will be blessed," I repeated. An understanding look passed between us, and we all went on, wayfarers that touched for a moment.

Over the winding path in the valley still hung the jungle fragrance of decaying vegetation, I breathed it with delight and felt gay of heart. We passed a little hut standing there solitary; by the well was a patch of rice cultivation; the sun shone on the sheet of water where the green shoots showed promisingly. Such a peaceful little settlement it looked, lying among the hills, the water in the stream rippling past, no bazaar smells or noises or crowds. "*Ayya!*" [1] I called in gaiety of spirit to the man standing in the doorway of the hut, "how happy are you! living all alone in this wilderness with only God for your neighbour."

"God for my neighbour," he repeated and turned straight round and disappeared into the hut.

A little disappointed, I walked on. Had he not understood? But perhaps—with incurable optimism this morning—he was busy. A shout behind made me turn my head. The man was dragging a string cot out of the hut. So *that* had been his instantaneous thought—to get a seat for the stranger! He beckoned imperiously. "Sit down, sit down," he said, as I came back, "talk some more."

But would he have responded so immediately if he had not already been feeling, though perhaps vaguely, what the

[1] Sir, or man, the ordinary mode of address.

unpremeditated sentence suddenly crystallized for him? One could picture his life. Arising every morning to the quiet beauty all around, thinking, no doubt, only of the waiting tasks of his little farm, yet the radiant dew, the deep shadow of the great trees at noon, the glow of evening, the sounds and silences among the rocky hills,—had they not, though hardly consciously to himself, carried a message and an appeal? And when one morning someone came past and said, "Didn't you know? That was God all the time," his awakened soul unfolded tender wings and said softly, "I knew it. Sit down, help me to understand some more."

"Great is the harvest." Is that the harvest He saw? In human hearts everywhere the hidden longing for God, waiting to be helped into consciousness? [1]

"The fields are white." Not only in ancient Samaritan towns, or in the heart of a woman of doubtful character long ago, but in Indian villages hidden away among hills, and in little solitary wayside farms, *to-day.*

[1] This thought is further developed in *The Way of Christ in the Harvest Field.* Christian Literature Society, Madras.

CHAPTER XIII

I AM carrying about another puling infant. It has been disturbing my night's rest for some time and claiming a good deal of attention during the day. We have started a Mohammedan school in this town.

The needs and possibilities in Bukkuru opened my eyes to the needs and possibilities in Andapur. A third of its population is Mohammedan and little or nothing is being done for them by anybody. The Municipality have a school for the boys, but the girls are entirely neglected. How to begin to get at them ? In Bukkuru a nice ready-made school was presented to me, so to speak; here in Andapur no such convenient offering seemed forthcoming. Consultation with Dorcas, our capable and courageous Biblewoman, enlisted her excellent business sense in the attack on the problem. She discovered Kasim Sahib, one of the few educated Mohammedans here. To my delighted surprise he evinced the utmost sympathy with my plans for his co-religionists. " I can supply you with a teacher," he offered, " my own sister." The walls of this Jericho seemed to be going down before a trumpet had been blown.

" Dorcas, let us find a house and rent it at once."

But here the tottering walls showed unexpected firmness. Andapur is crowded; wedged in between the large reservoir on one side and rice fields on the other there is no room for expansion; vacant houses are almost impossible to find.

Diligent search for one proved unsuccessful. But little difficulties, such as having no school building for a school, are not mountains in India, only mole-hills which may be jumped if they refuse to move. We started in a court-yard under a tree. Kadija Bi, the promised sister, brought six girls, and a beginning was made. Soon there were eight, twelve, twenty. No more could the yard hold. But the battle turned to the persistent—the little school and its needs became known and a house was *offered* to us. The room was soon so full I almost trod upon infants when I wormed my way in.

Kadija stood majestically in the midst of her kingdom with a ruler. "*Quamoosh!*"[1] she ejaculated from time to time, pointing the instrument at an unruly miscreant. As all of them were unruly miscreants her task was extensive. She varied it by standing by a more intelligent pupil and pointing out, *aliph*, *be*, *pe*, *te*, obediently repeated by the pupil, whom she interrupted by the peremptory "*Quamoosh!*" to the others. Kadija, in short, had no idea whatever of teaching. Moreover she was much too old to learn. No Inspectress worthy the name would recognize a school under such a teacher.

Many inquiries in every quarter I could think of produced a letter from my friend Mr. Rangavachari in Penuroy, recommending another Mohammedan woman who proved to be a much more efficient teacher, and with great gladness she was invited to Andapur. Kadija was thanked for her labours, and after due notice and payment according to contract her services were no longer required.

Next day there were hardly any children in the school. Without forethought I could put my feet down anywhere. Ungrateful for the freedom from the necessity to look before and after, I pined for what is not. "Ghaus Bi, what has happened?"

"Kadija has taken all the children to her house and is teaching them there," said the new teacher dolefully.

I flew round to Kasim Sahib. This must have been done without his knowledge. For many times he had said to me, "I know my sister is no good as a teacher. But to make a beginning with the school I will send her till you get

[1] "Be quiet!"

someone else. She is old too, and my wife wants her in the house." This I had believed, with the incurable simplicity of the West.

A cold reception awaited me, and a rough awakening. "Now that you are not employing my sister any more I do not take any interest in your school. If the children stay away they stay away. All *our* girls shall read at home."

Disillusioned and disappointed, I returned to the school and sought the conductress who brings the children to school.

"She has given notice," said the new teacher. "She will not come any more."

There we are now. But I am learning that, as in camp with transport and food and climatic difficulties, there is always a way out, so one can be found in school troubles. At least, I hope I am learning it; I confess that whenever a new mountain looms up I feel tempted to declare it to be immovable.

Dorcas tackled this one in her energetic way, gave Kadija Bi a piece of her mind and brought back the conductress and a number of children.

Hillocks, however, keep on appearing. Prejudices abound. To-day, again in that school, "seeing a great many who were not there," I went to their houses to catch the little truants. On my rounds I discovered curious reasons for absence. "In your reading-books," expostulated the parents, "you have pictures of a father and mother and child sitting together, why teach girls about babies and mothers, and put these things into their heads? Teach them Arabic and sacred words!" Evidently long prayers and incantations are the proper thing for children; a lesson on ordinary family life is not only far from religion but anathema. In vain I argued that mothers with babies could be seen at every yard in the bazaar street—did they think they never became visible to the children till they saw them in a picture? What they really object to in pictures is the fear that they are, or may be, idolatrous. Training of the eye, modern educational methods, are of no value in their opinion. The good old ways, Kadija's parrot teaching, for instance, are the thing.

Their last objection added insult to injury: "There is no room in your school." There is, alas! now. It is true that the school is miserably stuffy. But how to get a new building without bricks, or bricks without money, or building without a site ? The lack of room aggravates the struggle for cleanliness. And when the pupils are sent out to wash they come back all anyhow; and their hair! They are callous to my exhibition of a cleanly combed child and a higgledy-piggledy one and the question which of the two they like best. They point smilingly to the tidy one, but that is all the effect it has. The mothers say "We have not food enough for our stomachs, have we oil for the hair ?" Without oil, of course, it cannot be done. I have bought plain combs for the school, and they are always getting lost or stolen. These children are the proverbial little Turks! with but little courtesy or docility. When we have a better building and more room there will be some chance—yes, *when*, not if.

It is a relief to get into the Hindu school. The shining eager faces beguiled me for a long time. "Please, give us another sum, please just one more!" The imps recognize a fellow-feeling, I see ambition working in their faces, and remember a remote æon when the same thing worked frantically in myself. When mischief and naughtiness laugh at me from their eyes all the original sin in me hastens to laugh back; we are fellow-sinners, and they know it, and even sums are a joke.

To-day I missed my little *vigraham* [1] whose real and proud name is Nara Simha Rao (Man-Lion, one of the incarnations of Vishnu). I had met him first in his own home where he planted himself squarely in front of me as I sat talking with his mother.

[1] Idol, image.

"Missiamma!" he demanded attention.

"Brotherling!" I responded.

"Your school . . ." he struggled.

"Our school," I encouraged.

"I am coming to it!" he burst out with determination, evidently his little heart in both hands.

"Brotherling, as soon as you are a girl you may," I promised. But why not let little brothers come to school with their sisters? After all, permission was accorded. Since then he comes most days; sitting on the school bench generally mother-naked, his little legs crossed under him, radiant, fat, contented, unperturbed, with a smile so beaming and benignant that I surrendered at discretion the first time I saw him there. "Oh, golden Image!" I addressed him, and fell down and worshipped. "Missiamma's *vigraham*" is now his appellation at school and at home.

To-day the blessing of his little presence failed; he had fever, I was told, and presently I went the few doors away to his home to inquire. The mother's face wore an expression of deep anxiety. "Oh, it is not your *vigraham*," she explained in reply to my concerned question, "he has only a cold. I am so troubled about my daughter, your old pupil Sitamma who is now expecting her first baby. I am in great fear; did not Adi Lakshmi, my eldest daughter, die in her first confinement? I wanted Sita to come here, we sent many letters, even the money for her rail-fare; they made no reply and sent the money back, with a post card to say they had enough money themselves. She is in a small village; is there proper help there? Even in Bangalore Adi Lakshmi died. Oh, my poor daughter, two worlds, two great worlds, are between me and her!"

"Why don't you go to her, if she cannot come to you?" I asked.

She looked at me quite shocked. "It is not our custom. Always may we visit our sons, but not our daughters. Only if they specially ask you, and even then one must not stay longer than a day or two, though they press you."

I began to perceive. A mother, and a mother-in-law in one home—the situation might have its awkwardness.

"I do not even know if they are kind to her," the poor mother went on lamenting. "Why do they not write? Why don't they let her write? She always had much love for us, and now she is two worlds away"—the husband and mother-in-law I think constituted these—"and I am afraid, I think of Adi Lakshmi."

Poor mother—and poor Sita in that distant village, among evidently rather stern "in-laws"—no doubt thinking herself of her elder sister's fate and feeling frightened and lonely. It was not long since she had sat in our school, gay as the children this morning had been; she had the same sunny smile as my *vigraham*; is it being wiped off her face now, much, much too soon?

Women always have to go short in India whatever their status, I reflected; married, widowed, mothers, daughters. And as if waiting to confirm my thoughts, I noticed four Brahmin widows in their red garb, sitting in a verandah I passed. I knew the house. "Where is Venkamma?" I asked, "and the others?"

"Gone to the wedding. All gone to the wedding."

"Whose wedding?" I asked.

"My daughter's," was the reply from one of the shaved figures, looking up wistfully.

"Your daughter's!" I exclaimed, and just in time remembered to leave unspoken the words, "and you are here?" For she would not have liked the direct allusion to her widowhood which forbade her presence on such an auspicious occasion. But—her own daughter's wedding!

"How is your daughter?" I turned to the next widow.

"She had a son last week!" said the grandmother proudly. "But she had much fever, I wait for news; there is only an old aunt in the house to help."

"And here you sit doing nothing," I swallowed my words again. Well I knew she was eating her heart out to go to her child. But—a widow present at a birth! Even if there were no one else to help a mother may not look after her own child if she is so unfortunate as to be widowed herself.

How hardly and even cruelly the various results of India's thought of women press on their hearts and lives! Who can make them free but Christ?

Meanwhile there were my own burdens to shoulder; Dorcas awaited me at home. The Mohammedan owner of the room rented for our school sent us a month's notice. I expect it is intended to extort a bigger rent; still, it may be sincere, as houses are difficult to obtain. In either case it means difficulty.

A disturbance in the verandah—Eliza, the wife of a pensioned Christian police bugler, staggered in crying and sobbing as if all her world had come to an end, begging for justice. Her husband was away; Sundra Lal, a Christian clerk, was in the habit of visiting their home. That morning he had called while she had had some jewellery out for cleaning, notably a gold ring; Sundra Lal admired it, tried it on and did not give it back. She sat sewing, saying once or twice, "Give it me back," and he replied, "Yes, directly." She had to go into her kitchen for a moment; before she returned, he had left the house, ring and all. She followed him to his house asking for the ring back. "But I gave it to you," he said, "when you were sewing," and maintains this story. I can neither believe Sundra Lal capable of such a thing, nor Eliza of inventing it all. Intuition is entirely at fault. Yet the ring has gone. "Lend me the money to make a new one before my husband comes back," cried Eliza, "he will kill me if he finds it gone."

The post arrived adding its quota to the riddles before me. A neighbouring Mission wrote that one of our young teachers in training there had got into trouble with a middle-aged widow. They believed the latter was chiefly to blame;

the young man's career should not be ruined; yet discipline must be maintained; how can his training continue?

Catechist Joel wrote asking what was to be done about Jivamma, betrothed to a Hindu before her parents became Christians; she is of marriageable age, but does not want to go to the Hindu who is indifferent to her and has taken a concubine.

An anonymous letter accused Dharmpalli Prema of abortion, and the teacher of being the cause; Prema, who is to be married next month to another man! No notice is ever taken of anonymous letters; yet the mud thrown leaves a smudge.

It is hard sometimes not to feel sickened, or become tired in spirit, hard to keep on making allowances for a low stage of development and to handle these things with a patient and hopeful heart. The courage of God ever to start on this universe at all amazes me daily more; to expect people to choose goodness! To have the patience to wait for things to grow, and take the risk of their growing all crooked!

* * * * *

But moods of despondency may be put to flight suddenly. To-day my corner of the globe was invaded by unexpected light. The mail arrived, and since then I have been singing psalms and hymns—for it brought from a friend of Missions £100 at one fine swoop, for building a Mohammedan school; is it not a miracle?

(I wonder if the angels are laughing at our fussy faith. So astonished are we when a little money is produced. They can do more difficult things than that for us!)

It happened when I had been mourning; for when an appeal went home I had pinned my faith to the Arthington fund. Then came the dismal information that Arthington had specially excluded all Mohammedan work. Down went my spirits, as if the divine resources were pinned to the Arthington fund also. At the moment I could preach a fine sermon on this theme!

CHAPTER XIV

The thrills of daily life go on. In the Mohammedan school sickness has occasioned a vacancy; an applicant for it has just left the verandah. This was the interview.

Manager: " I see you have been Urdu *munshi.* Can you give other lessons ? "

Applicant: " I know all the subjects."

Manager: " Nature lessons, for instance ? "

Applicant: " I know all the subjects."

Manager: " How would you give a lesson on—let me see—on a leaf ? " presenting the applicant with one plucked from a plant in the verandah.

Applicant (*receiving it with hesitation*): " A leaf. . . . Hm, a leaf; rrhm, a tree has leaves. Rrhm. A tree has roots also. Hm, rrhm, rrrrrhm." (Glances were directed at the manager who was busy imitating a pupil's stare of attention.) " A tree sticks in the ground by its roots." (Further glances at stonily silent manager. Bright idea occurred.) " There are also seeds. If you sow a seed there will be another tree. . . ." Pause. More pause; manager gazing skywards.

Applicant (*desperately*): " Leaves are green."

Unbroken pause. Manager (*relenting*): " Perhaps a leaf is a little difficult. Let us try another. An easy one—let us see; the cow. How would you give a lesson about the cow ? "

Applicant (*greatly relieved, stepped briskly forward*): " I show a picture of a cow to the children."

Pause. The manager mentally gazed at the picture and sat expectant.

Applicant: " The cow has one head, one tail, four legs." Pause. (Ha, yes, of course.) " The cow gives milk. The cow is a very useful animal."

The flow ceased. The manager waited. Relenting at last: " What does the cow eat ? "

APLICANT (*in eager gratitude and haste*): " Grass! The cow eats grass. Also straw. *Cholum* straw. Straw. Grass."

MANAGER: " What happens after eating ? "

APPLICANT (*joyfully*): " It gives milk! "

MANAGER: " Can you tell me anything about the digestive arrangements of a cow ? "

Applicant was rendered speechless by the manager's indelicacy.

MANAGER (*casually*): " I suppose the cow has a stomach."

APPLICANT (*wonderingly*): " Yes, the cow has a stomach."

MANAGER (*severely*): " It has four. . . ."

APPLICANT (*hastily, the light of remembrance breaking in upon him*): " Yes, yes, four stomachs! One full of milk, one full of juice, one full of blood. . . ." But the manager interrupted sternly.

" Let us take geography. What would you teach about . . . yes, about Asia ? "

APPLICANT (*looking frantically at the ceiling for help*): " Asia. Asia."

MANAGER (*getting tired*): " Do you know of any countries in Asia ? "

APPLICANT: "Yes, I know. India, Australia, Mesopotamia."

MANAGER (*interested*): " Any more ? "

APPLICANT: " Bassorah, Bagdad, Kut el Amara."

" It's an ill wind that blows no one any good," reflected the manager. " Even world wars have their uses! "

Yet our need is so great, inspection being before the doors —the Christian teacher is ill in hospital—that he and his wife were engaged to fill the gap.

* * * * *

The day before inspection I entered the school. Abdul, the Pompous, sat there, but no others.

" I should like to see the Teachers' Attendance Register," I asked, glancing at the unshepherded classes.

" Please excuse me, I left it at home."

" But why did you take it away ? "

" I took it by mistake on Saturday."

This being Monday the slip was allowed to pass. " What nature-study lesson will you give in the inspection ? "

" The elephant."

" Shall we have it now ? "

" Hm, rrhm, ahem. . . . STAND! " The class stood.

" Without a picture ? " I whispered softly.

" Child, bring a picture of an elephant! " majestically.

" You will remember, won't you, to-morrow, that a teacher should have ready all he needs for a lesson ? " I whispered again.

" Oh, ah, ah, yes. . . . I shall bring."

Children, returning from fruitless quest: " There is no picture of an elephant."

TEACHER (*hastily casting a roving eye along the school walls and spotting the picture of a camel*): " I will take the camel. STAND! '

The picture was placed before the class. " The camel. C-a-m-e-l." " C-a-m-e-l," repeated the children obediently.

" It lives in a sandy country, Arabia. Nowhere else."

MANAGER (*sotto voce*): " Egypt, Soudan, Sahara."

TEACHER (*also sotto voce*): " But they are in Arabia."

MANAGER: " No, Africa."

TEACHER: " The camel lives in Arabia and Africa."

Here the manager went off to find a map and perceived a book on the top of the cupboard. It turned out to be the missing Teachers' Attendance Register, evidently hastily hidden there. The absent women teachers, one of whom was Abdul's wife, were marked present!

" The teachers must be fined for absence without leave," I remarked; the man responded with enthusiasm, " I recommend them for a fine." The woman teacher who is not his wife came up sobbing to the house afterwards, and explained she had a sick child and no one to go for medicine, of this she had informed the head teacher and asked for leave, but no such word of excuse escaped him; he was only too thankful to see the storm gathering not over his head alone! Later I went round to the inspecting officer to warn her that she will either lose her temper or her gravity, and in either case her self-control, when she hears that lying fossil teach. With what gratitude and humility shall I welcome the Christian teacher when she returns from hospital!

I asked the Mohammedan pupils where were the leaflets I had given. (These are separately printed Scripture portions.) Nowhere. Had they learned them? No. But when I was beginning to assert inwardly "I say the struggle nought availeth" Hussein Bi told me that they had been taken home, some fathers had seen them, shown them to neighbours, read them to admiring and respectful audiences and kept them reverently. "I believe they think it is the Koran," said Hussein Bi. My poor little Mohammedan school, with no Christian teachers just now, so you are making a little evangelizing effort of your own?

* * * * *

Mr. Abdul Kareem has left; but the Christian teacher, alas! had to undergo a second operation which means another three months' absence. Another Mohammedan woman teacher has been found who can take the higher standards; in the lower ones I still beat myself against a rock. "The children are so stupid," is always the teacher's excuse; triumphantly she witnessed my failure with colours. "Show me something red," I asked the class.

"Show me something red," they repeated dully.

I wheeled. "Do they do any work in your house?"

"Do they . . ." began the parrots, but one or two said, "They sweep."

"How?" I pounced.

"Like this."

"Let us all sweep," they were invited; and we all swept.

"What else do they do?" A little eagerness awoke.

"They pound."

"How?"

"Let us all pound."

In the end, at the word of command, we pounded, swept, ground grain, drew water, carried it, washed clothes, blew the fire, winnowed, etc. The discouraging thing is that this kind of thing had been shown the teachers before. They are middle-aged women, rather tired and buffeted by life; the energy required, the mental adaptability, are no longer in them. Always and everywhere comes the reflection that all these things have to be taught when young.

The new teacher, though younger and more energetic, already showed the parrot habit that seems so deeply ingrained. Composition was to rouse the minds of the pupils into agility. I found that instead of making them exercises in thinking she had caused a few themes to be learned by heart!

With inveterate hopefulness the more excellent way was once more upheld.

"What has that girl got in her pocket?" I asked, pointing to a bulge in a little jacket. We all wondered. We all stared unblinkingly. The proud owner, not averse to act the universally beloved part of showman, began to pull out the contents. Not one of us had any other interest in life than to watch what came out. A dirty, dog-eared booklet. A rag. Half an inch of pencil. A quarter of an anna. Greedily the coin was seized.

"What is that?"

"A *bottu*!"

"What is the good of it?"

"We can get something for it."

"Where?"

"In shops." To shops we resorted, buying the most

incredible things at the most wonderful prices, *bottus* became rupees, houses and gardens and cattle came within our reach, the sweets we obtained made our mouths water; we bought cloth for jackets and skirts, and cotton and silk for embroidery, feminine interest stirred all round; for the millionth time a poor manager wished that there was nothing for her to do but schools!

Scripture lessons followed. Here we sometimes have resort to somewhat unsabbatic methods.

" Shall we act the silly sheep again ? " the children volunteered; without waiting for permission they began to distribute rôles. " I'll say, ' Don't run away.' " " I will say, ' No, that is not our shepherd calling, that is a robber,' " " I will say, ' Do you see that creature like a dog ? It is a wolf ' " —a threatening storm of " Baa, baa, baa ! " arose.

" No, let us take something smaller to-day."

" A dog ? A rat ? A squirrel ? A bird ? A fly ? "

" No, no, no. Still smaller." At last we hit upon it. An ant. We crawled over the floor like ants and talked ant language by knocking our heads when we met; we discovered and picked up food, carried it to holes where other ants were waiting; we put out little eggs in the sun, we shoo'ed away strangers; we discovered it takes a great deal to be as wise as an ant! Finally we searched for a real one—never far away in Indian plains—put it carefully in the middle of an admiring circle, and a child beside it. While one of the objects sat in state like an idol, the other showed a tendency to bolt; still, we had a chance to bethink ourselves which was the more excellent creature and to draw the conclusion that a Creator who taught the ant such wisdom was likely to be educating us also towards some high purpose. That was our lesson; if not doctrinal, neither was it dull! And who can tell what is going on in the soul of a child at moments of happiness and receptivity ?

* * * * *

A more advanced process of education in thinking is persisted in in the Telugu school which holds a mixture of Christian and Hindu girls. In the daily Bible lessons results were at first something like this. " What do you know of Stephen ? " " He preached and he was killed by the enemies." Gradually a bit soaked in. " To serve tables you need the help of God's spirit to do it properly," said several when asked to draw a lesson for ourselves. Hopefully I gave Standards VII and VIII, all Christian girls, the whole of Acts vii. to read through, but when I asked, " What is it all about ? " I had only puzzled faces. " Moses," ventured one. I admit Stephen was a little discursive, and the Telugu version is by no means very plain; so that my hope of hearing " Stephen's sermon and his death " showed but my own incompetence as a teacher in expecting children to perceive essentials in a mass of details. However, we all forgave one another, and attacked the problem of essentials. But when next day I asked, " What was the main point in Stephen's address ? " only silence answered me. Then came ventures slithering beside the mark, " He was one of seven," " He was filled with the Spirit," " He saw heaven opened," " He was stoned "—it was as if they said, " We like a story; and why must we think ? "

But a relentless manager held their poor little minds to the grindstone.

" Who are the people who think they know the way of salvation ? "

" Christians."

" And formerly ? "

After much roundabout elicitation: " The Jews."

" And what did they do with their knowledge ? " More elicitation.

" And if Christians don't use *their* knowledge ? "

Children sat awestruck. But I daresay in my eagerness to point a moral I have muddled them again! Never do I get an answer to the "think questions" that are continued to be flung at them; such as "When the Christians were persecuted and had to flee was there any advantage in their being dispersed?" or "The Samaritans became Christians. Can you give me any illustrations how Christianity breaks down barriers in this country as it did of old between Jews and Samaritans?" Not a bit of it. Yet there they sat—illustrations in themselves.

Not one of them, when they had read the story of Cornelius failed to mention the words, "One Simon, surnamed Peter"—the importance of names has manifestly been well drilled into them in other lessons, though even then they did not realize it was Peter of the Gospels. But when I burst myself in the effort to show the greatness of the advance of admitting a "heathen," not a Jew, and asked for a moral, it was one girl out of twenty-eight who remembered something about Christianity breaking down caste distinctions.

So easily the world takes the results of battles fought long ago!

CHAPTER XV

PRESSURE becomes at times so heavy that life seems a veritable car of juggernaut. The worst consequence is that the inner life suffers and there seems no time to replenish it; sometimes I sigh for the former years when early morning walks were possible and when I could put up altars under many a green tree or shady rock.

I have been reading Catherine of Siena's life at mealtimes, and the importance of the inward activities is freshly forced upon me. But I cannot spend hours in prayer and meditation; days are full from morning till night. Did, perhaps, these saints gain, with difficulty, a heritage not only for themselves but for us, us who have to possess it under modern conditions, without rapt devotions and ecstasies; beset, instead, by common claims and duties, and learning to endure *there*? Yet, surely, their insistence and their practice is significant for us; the high road of prayer they followed calls to us to tread it also, if we would know what they knew. Whence it came that my early morning found me out on the plain by a grey rock; everything else looked grey also in the monsoon weather; perhaps my soul did too.

" My peace I give unto you." Is not that an even greater miracle than healing a cripple? to transform something intangible, delicate, evasive, like a tired heart or a sick spirit, into a healthy and serene one more wonderful than to transform sick tissues into sound ones? What materialists we all are, and how out of perspective our standards remain.

Rumours are flying about of cholera having broken out in the villages around. When I visited with Dorcas in the afternoon the significant waterpot stood in the verandah where we sat talking; the refreshment for " the Mother," i.e. the cholera goddess who flies round at night and seeks entrance into houses. She might be getting tired and about to rest in this verandah (which would mean death for the inmates), so this pot is to induce her to drink and gain strength to go farther. When I saw this pathetic sign of fear, the meditation of the morning came back. " My peace I give unto you." Words spoken with the certainty of death approaching. Here also was fear of death approaching, but, alas! no peace.

A Brahmin woman was looking over the low wall of the next courtyard, listening. Suddenly she interrupted.

" You speak from here "—touching her heart—" not from here," pointing to her lips.

I gazed at her dumbfounded. That that woman's heart should almost instantly comprehend that she was listening to a message very hardly won by the speaker! " Yes, your words come from deep down," she nodded; and, as I still gazed at her in silence, " why do you look at me like that? Do you think I am mad ? "

" No, no," I recovered myself. " I am glad you understand. Will you not take this way ? "

" Ah, it is a very high way," she replied. " Our people are not fit. We have not merit like you."

* * * * *

Andapur is raging with cholera. Cases occurred near the Mohammedan school which had to be closed. The Telugu school was still going, but yesterday the new headmaster, Sudarsanam, who is doing excellently, sent a note at midday to say he felt unwell; would I send medicine. A little later came another note saying he could not go to afternoon school. I cycled down and found little Shantamma bravely holding the fort alone, and went on to the headmaster's house. A scene of horrible trouble met me. In one room lay poor Sudarsanam in cholera cramps; in the next lay his brother

David, also ill. In the courtyard their sister Jivi rent the air with shrieks. Sudarsanam's wife Ruth and her mother Leah were sitting by the wall miserable and nervous, because suffering from diarrhœa. Jivi's shrieks distracted everybody; I told her if she were not quiet I would lock her up in some other house. Ruth was brave and collected and set to to boil water. I raced to hospital on the cycle for disinfectants. On return it was going from one patient to the other, giving medicines, fomenting the stomach, rubbing extremities with turpentine and camphor; trying mustard plasters; in between a rush was made to the bungalow for barley water, for the thirst is frightful—all the while hoping for the promised visit of the doctor and saline injections. But he never came, there were too many calls elsewhere. The round from patient to patient went on, varied by hushing Jivi who had relapses, into quiet again, upholding the spirits of poor Ruth (who is within two months of her confinement) and talking myself hoarse to impress old Dan and Leah, Ruth's parents, with the absolute necessity of everybody using boiled water only and of keeping plenty ready. We went on till between nine and ten at night. I did not like the look of Sudarsanam; of David I had hopes, he yelled so lustily and was always fighting over something; at times I had to hold him down; "I must get out," he shrieked, "no air, no air!" though the monsoon wind was blowing in at the door. After a recent touch of fever I was exhausted by then; arranging with Raja Shekara, the headmaster of our boys' school, to stay the night, I returned home. It was nearly midnight before I got to bed; anxiety drove me forth between five and six in the morning, only to learn that Sudarsanam had died in the night. An urgent wire was sent for Joel to come to our help; I searched for wooden cases to be made into a coffin. In the stricken household no one was able to see to things, and there was no one else; the town is distracted with fear and with tragedies. Raja Shekara had inspection in his school to-day, of all days! So he had to be there. It was fairly terrible in the house of death. Cries of despair and sorrow resounded all the time; every one was worn out with the night's vigil; poor David was still between life and death; Leah still ill with diarrhœa and Ruth's little daughter Rani beginning; Ruth exhausted with weeping, and Jivi loudly lamenting that she was falling sick; the only quiet one was poor dead Sudarsanam. Ruth was induced to take some nourishment, then to go and rest in the house of a friendly neighbour; the rest were dosed with medicine (the baby forcibly) fresh barley water was made; fresh gruel; the whole courtyard disinfected, fresh bran ordered, then came interviews with gravediggers; the old father who might have helped to see about these things had been drinking to console himself; the rest were dazed with fatigue and grief. Dorcas was a brick; she had been up all night with them, but stayed all day also without rest; for David still needed the most careful attention. She is a dear, reliable, and unselfish woman. To my intense relief Joel arrived at midday; so here was someone to look after David, and to conduct the burial. By four o'clock the coffin was ready; I went to the house before it came to ensure quiet if possible, but found an impossible scene; the courtyard full of a crowd to whom a funeral remains a *tamasha*; Ruth had given way and was hanging over the corpse loudly wailing, her mother also, Jivi also—a few Christian women stood quietly weeping in the background; my own composure was threatened. The mortally sick David begged so pitifully to see his brother again that no one had the heart to forbid the men carrying him in to see Sudarsanam in his coffin. After a short service in the courtyard the body was carried out; I stayed to soothe the wailing women and presently on the cycle caught up the burial party. So we laid him to rest, " in sure and certain hope of the resurrection "—the monsoon wind shrieking round us and whirling up dust in the grey plain beyond; when the earth rattled down I could have sobbed. He had looked so lifelike; they had dressed him as he always was, I almost expected him to get up and tell me about some girl who had gone to the Government school. But yesterday he was at his post in full vigour. His parents arrived in the evening when the funeral was over; almost by main force I kept them in my compound; for the bereaved household must at all costs rest to-night; Ruth is threatening miscarriage, and if the parents went now it would mean talking and weeping all night. The poor people were almost beyond control with the suddenness of the sorrow, their wails rent the compound. It was only by representing to them the absolute necessity of consoling the poor widow and saving her coming baby, and encouraging the son still left to them, that they grew quieter at last and began to grasp that by such wild lamentations they were in a fair way of killing the others. I thought it safer to accompany them next morning to ward off these nerve-racking demonstrations of grief, but I am thankful to say they came in quietly.

There was little time for condolence; every one had to be dosed, and food prepared for David and little Rani who is of the most obstinate temperament and rejected it vigorously, but had to yield in the end! It made a wholesome distraction in the terribly sorrow-laden air; so also did curt speech to old Dan, for in spite of all admonitions he brought the child unboiled water; Jivi also incurred wrath, after teaching her till my eyes streamed in the smoke, how to make gruel I watched her from the door making the next lot and saw her take it off the fire the moment it boiled. "Does raw rice turn into cooked rice for one minute's bubbling? Will not raw flour poison your brother?" The wonder is they live at all with such shiftless ways.

* * * * *

Andapur is blazing at the four corners with cholera now—terrible tragedies occur. A Christian official from here took his wife and children to Bangalore; on the Andapur station the children started cholera symptoms; the ten hours' journey was a nightmare of horror, at the destination the poor father carried the two children, still alive but insensible to the house, as no cart would take them. Shortly after, the eldest, a lovely little boy of four, died. Only a few days ago he had had a ride on my cycle, sparkling with life and joy. This thing is awful in its suddenness. A neighbour of Samuel went to his field in the morning, at nine he returned feeling ill, at eleven they carried out his corpse.

It is now in the Police Lines next door to us. People's terror greatly increases the danger; we let it be known that anyone could get medicine here. I had to lay in a good stock, as the hospital supplies were so quickly exhausted. Now I am rather overrun by people with symptoms, most of the latter sheer nervousness, for after a dose they promptly stop. I went through the lines this morning, " Ho, everyone that is afraid! Take a drop of this and you will not fall ill! " swallowing a drop myself in front of them. " Yes, it is a certain preventive," I assured them boldly, as numbers crowded round. " Take it and live! " As confidence is half the battle I hope that in the lines at all events the enemy is kept at bay.

* * * * *

I was unpacking a fresh batch of medicines when at my window appeared a face, Khalak, the husband of my little new teacher in the Mohammedan school. " Zainab is ill." I seized one of the bottles and whisked down to town. " Ten times diarrhœa! " she moaned. " No vomiting, no cramps? " I asked. " Oh come, Zainab Bi, take this medicine; here is gruel for you, you are all right."

" Zainab much worse," came Khalak's voice again at

my window a couple of hours later. "She is very weak." "Is this a new kind of cholera?" I thought desperately in my lay ignorance as I cycled down again. There she lay and could hardly whisper; she is a delicate little thing and might go out like a breath. From twelve to four I sat and spoon-fed her, during which time there was not a single recurrence. Then Dorcas was left in charge for some hours, gruel and broth made at the bungalow were sent to her. Next morning I found the cat had had the gruel, and as the flies had been allowed to settle on the broth (containing the main portion of a pot of Brand's essence!) they had thrown it away. Instead of having had all that nourishment Zainab Bi had gone without any, was fearfully weak in consequence, and the old symptoms back in force. Everything had to be made afresh, she was left dosed, fed, cheered, provided; and I set off on my morning's round.

"Zainab *very* bad now, great pains in the stomach!" Khalak's face and voice at my window again. This time I set to with mustard plaster and fomentations to get the pains relieved; also I broke out in wrath, for I found the gruel they had made nothing but lumps. With streaming eyes I cooked another over their smoking wood fire, since they must learn (Khalak really has now), and after fussing over her for an hour she was better again. "When I see you there I feel as if I were not ill at all," said Zainab with a wan smile, but when you go I feel frightened." So there I was glued a hot sticky midday long to keep the little goose from feeling frightened. But alas, how your best actions are misinterpreted! I thought I had been plain about instructions for the night—"Let the patient rest and sleep if sleep comes; if awake and restless feed at intervals"; but what are words against actions? Khalak, who had watched mine through the midday, woke up poor Zainab who would have slept beautifully every hour to feed her; and again she was weak and ill! Meanwhile there was a rain of urgent wires from her relatives to whom Khalak had wired that she had cholera (which I think she was within an ace of having from sheer fright). And now her baby is getting sore eyes.

I could not go to her for some hours to-day; the *maistry* was waiting—the workmen are going on strike because of the cholera; I had to go and harangue them; after an hour's talk they promised to work *one more day*! The widow of a teacher at Dharmpalli who died of cholera came to bewail her present and inquire of me her future fate; a number of other time-traps caught me fast; when I went back to Zainab in the evening the symptoms were worse than ever, and she was as weak as a kitten. That settled it; I packed her up and brought her to the bungalow, where she is installed now, and apparently cured *instanter*! The way the transfer wrought magic was almost ridiculous; in her house I could venture on nothing but liquids; here, it seemed it was safe to give her almost anything; she had solid food without ill consequences. It is satisfactory that a Mission bungalow is as good as the Ganges is said to be, destructive of cholera germs and any other evil microbes!

Zainab is an educated girl who talks English well; I feel as if I had suddenly got a daughter; at table she jabbers away and I hear many things. The child of a wealthy merchant, the only girl after several brothers, she seems to have been fearfully spoilt at home. These notions persisted after marriage.

" Oh, Miss Sahiba, shall I tell you how foolish I was? It was shortly after my marriage; my husband had been out walking; his nice silk coat was caught in a thorn-bush and a little torn. When he came in he asked very politely if I would mend it. I said, yes, but Miss Sahiba, I cried all night! I would not eat my meals; I would not speak to anyone; my brother came, my husband, all stood round and asked me what was the matter. I said 'nothing,' but went on being miserable. At last my youngest brother begged me privately to tell him my trouble. I said, ' My husband asked me to mend his coat. *Am I a tailor?* Do I do low work like that ? ' "

Meal-times, which I thought might be a little difficult, are proving unexpectedly entertaining.

Zainab's younger brother became a Christian and drew her after him, though she is not yet baptized. In a real, though at times childish way, she is very much in earnest.

Cholera still scourges the whole district; news came from Bukkuru of terrible times there; Giriappa's wife fell ill, but recovered; then his Hindu brother, who died. Radha was seized—I heard this together with the news that she was safely over the worst and thanked God.

But to-day a great sorrow has befallen; her sister, our beloved Prema, has gone. She hurried in from Marala when she heard Radha was ill, though herself suffering from fever. In this weakened state she nursed her sister through cholera, then fell ill herself and, without warning, passed away. I cannot yet believe I shall never see her again in this life; I loved her, I think, above the others; hers was one of the humblest and sweetest spirits I have ever known. *Never* once have I heard her say a sharp word, or a complaining one, or one derogatory of someone else; never have I seen her face anything but sunshiny, peaceful, and loving; I hardly know of what other human being one could say that.

I remember her courage when she was first asked to go to Marala; there were no other Christians there except the recently baptized Naramma of Bukkuru, who had gone to live there with her relatives. No one would let a house to a Christian—at last Naramma prevailed upon her people, the potters, to allow Prema a portion of their room. It held no privacy or conveniences; a baby on the other side of the low partition cried all night; access from outside was by a doorway over which she hung a mat as there was no door; every time she went out she had to carry her belongings next door for security. Baths could only be taken in a neighbour's house; yet of all these daily small hardships she never said one complaining word. (When I discovered them, those within my reach, such as a door, a bath-place, were remedied.) Meanwhile she won such love and respect in the village that when a house belonging to one of the chief men became vacant he of his own accord offered it to Prema.

This dear woman had not the gifts of her sister; but she loved much. I always cherished the hope that in the Home for girls and women here that I ceaselessly dream of she would be the head. She would have been no disciplinarian, but I think she would have diffused a spirit of love and peace better that any discipline. Instead, she has gone on; of the two Christians who wrote neither said "she died," only "she has reached the presence of the Lord."

Yes, she has arrived where she always was at home.

CHAPTER XVI

THE bungalow is an accomplished fact, I am writing from the upstairs verandah with its outlook over the little garden and the windy plain to a horizon of rocky hills. Here I sit and gloat over the great Babylon that I have built. In the town the new Mohammedan school building rears a red-tiled gable over the surrounding mud roofs; while it was being built plague invaded our district; rats died in the town; the authorities ordered the whole place to be evacuated. Many people fled, huts and sheds arose on the *maidans* around for those who remained; workmen and building materials became locally unobtainable; entrance to the town was only allowed by special permit. The struggles with building difficulties alone would fill a fat volume, and schools themselves remain a perpetual struggle. Last week I went round to our new institution in the Town Extension and sat down by Susan's class during her Bible lesson. A little pupil was relating the lesson learnt. "Jesus sat in the house of a *Shastri*.[1] A poor woman who was bad came near and cried. The people said she should not come near and cry. But Jesus said, 'She is a poor woman, let her be. You must not trouble a poor woman.'"

Presently I questioned Susan privately. It was all she remembered herself. She had not troubled to read that incomparable story over beforehand.

"No wonder the Educational Department demands notes of lessons," I sighed.

The quality of our teachers is an unceasing puzzle. Though, may be, we are much too hasty in the standards we apply, Susan's own parents were raw and shiftless *Malas*; she was one of the first girls from our district to be educated.

[1] Scholar, scribe.

That she should be here now, teaching little high caste children anything at all is surely no mean progress.

I turned to a Brahmin teacher's class. "What is your lesson?"

"The earth and its revolutions."

"Very good. Please ask them what you have taught."

The Brahmin eyed his class sternly. "Does the earth go round?"

"Yes, oh yes," responded the children cheerfully.

"How do you know?" probed the teacher. "Can you prove it?"

No, they could not. Privately I thought the proof had been beyond the power of a Galileo even, but vaguely hoped that modern teaching might be more advanced.

"Have I not told you," the teacher scolded the class, "that you know the earth turns round; that it is just like when we go in the train, with all our luggage and ink bottles and books and sit down and shut the door and then we fly along. Now, how do you know the earth moves?"

"We go in the train," repeated docile parrots, "with our luggage, and ink bottles, and shut the door and fly along."

I drew the teacher aside. "What on earth do you mean? You asked the children to give some proof that the earth revolves."

"Yes. It is a parable. We go in the train with all our luggage and ink bottles. . . ."

"Never mind about the luggage," I interrupted; temper beginning to fray a little.

"We go in the train," the teacher proceeded in his fixed groove, "with all our luggage and ink bottles and books, and sit down and shut the door and then we fly along."

The hopelessness of phrases repeated hundreds of times became apparent, also the hopelessness of trying to replace them by reason in a lazy and, by this time, impervious mind.

"But what you are saying is sheer nonsense," I said, trying after all to pierce his mental rind.

"I learned it like that in the training and read it in books," protested the injured teacher. "If you affirm it is not so what can I say?"

I spared a thought of impatience for "the training." The everlasting piling on of undigested facts, and still less digested illustrations! We need remodelled training schools where the chief end of man and woman shall be to be made to think for themselves.

The next class emphasized precisely the same thing. Here also geography was in progress. The teacher was a rather glib young woman.

"I have been telling the children the proofs that the earth is round," she informed me.

"I should like to hear them," I replied, settling myself, though no words can express how sick I am of the proofs of the earth being round. If I could by any means pound the thing into a rectangular pulp, I would. If only to get the teachers to think!

"If an ant crawls round an orange," a pupil began fluently, "it would come back to the same spot. This proves the earth is round."

"Any more proofs?" I inquired with awakening interest.

"When a ship travels on the sea it sees first the topyard of another ship. This proves the earth is round."

"And when we go in trains," broke in the next pupil eagerly, "we see the telegraph wires go up and down. This proves the earth is round."

I was certainly learning something. The teacher seemed complacently pleased at the ready answers and glanced at me for appreciation. I don't know what I looked like, but it put her on the defensive.

"We learned it like that in the training and I read it in a book," she said hesitatingly.

We certainly need a modern training school badly. But it would have to be a first-class one. It is not a piece of work that could be done by a missionary already in charge of half a dozen other pieces of work, "with Indian help." Until certain ingredients of character are possessed by a larger number of men and women within the Christian community, the Indian teachers in such a training school are not likely to be very much better than the present teachers in ordinary schools. These things take time to grow, they must be part of the communal life, not only a possession of individuals here and there.

We are handicapped by the general character of the Telugu and Kanarese people; they are gentle and friendly and lovable but lacking in backbone; farther south the Tamils are a different race; less docile, less ready to please, more turbulent and riotous, but with how much grit! In the new Town Extension School the teacher never could produce any but the most languid drill and *kolatum* [1]; a little Tamil pupil arrived one day and transformed that *kolatum* in a few days into a performance of many new intricacies, carried out with precision, simply by illustrating how they did things in Tamil schools.

In our Church life we are faced with similar difficulties. Responsibility is being transferred to the Indian Church in all our stations; here in Andapur we have reorganized ourselves upon the same lines. Deacons have been elected, amongst them the woman missionary. At a recent meeting the secretary mentioned that a certain man was asking for baptism.

"Is he sincere?" I inquired.

"No, he is bad."

"Bad? Altogether? Why then does he want baptism? What makes you say he is bad?"

"He stole Anandam's turban."

[1] A kind of folk dancing.

"Well, he might have fallen into sudden temptation and still not be wholly bad; what were the circumstances? Anandam is not omniscient; it might be a mistake. Has the man been asked about it?"

Evidently he had not; they shifted their ground. "He does not come to church regularly."

"Perhaps his zeal grew cold. Should we try and revive it?"

"Are we then to call in thieves and all and sundry?"

"I am only saying that sometimes good desires grow cold again. Have we not all this experience?"

"Oh, if you wish it so much—all right; we must call him."

The judicial faculty is as yet undeveloped. Fairness, analysis of motives, allowances for faults have still to grow. The difficulty of avoiding personal feeling seems insuperable. "I think him bad, on such and such grounds. You don't accept my grounds? It shows you think nothing of *me*." It becomes a nice question for the European to what lengths he is to go in retiring into the background and allowing individuals to be sacrificed to inexperience.

Our dear Raja Shekara, who is now pastor of the church, is getting a taste of disappointing and unreliable people and sometimes feels rather discouraged. For instance, a deacons' meeting was called. The secretary did not turn up, but sent in his resignation. The rest of us looked blankly at one another, as we had no idea of the reason. A guess was hazarded that he might be hurt because the notice of the meeting did not go through him. "The pastor got up the meeting," said a deacon chivalrously, shifting the blame on Raja Shekara.

"I will apologize," said that man of lovely humility. "I will officially apologize." It turned out that he had talked about the meeting with the secretary, thought it was settled, and arranged details himself, instead of through the secretary.

This was certainly a slip—a slip against Red Tape—*Gott strafe* Red Tape! For this, though he had done it in good faith and without any other idea but of being helpful, he was ready to abase himself to any extent if that would mend matters. It did in the end; the secretary was appeased.

The position of pastor remains no sinecure. None is readier to serve others in any capacity than Raja Shekara, and our Christians are not slow to take advantage of him. They always send for him when sick, but not to minister spiritually. They ask him to save them the long walk to hospital and himself fetch medicine for them; they expect him to do much of the nursing and to sit up all night with a patient. They think because they contribute to his salary that they have a right to his whole time and can even order him about. They are not, perhaps, the first people to have that sort of notion! It reminded me of another Indian Church where the elders had the brilliant idea of fining their pastor eight annas because they had not liked his sermon!

Already the difficulty of men being unwilling to serve in the Indian Church is looming on the horizon. "We would rather work under the Mission."

Schools, teachers, congregations, pastors, churches, as well as missionaries have a slow and difficult and steep ascent before them in India.

CHAPTER XVII

INDIA is a land of many contrasts, not only in the physical but in the spiritual realm. At the present moment there are devastating floods and equally devastating droughts in the same district in the south. Some visitors I had to-day illustrated equally strong contrasts.

A few weeks ago Kaironesa, our new Mohammedan mistress, had asked for leave, as she had had a wire from her sister in Hyderabad to say she was ill of plague. When I returned from schools this morning I found her husband waiting for me in the verandah. He is a man with an English education, making his living by selling spectacles. He was in a fine frenzy about his wife; why had she gone away ? Her sister was quite well again, he began.

" But here is a wire to say the sister is worse and she cannot come yet," I interpolated. In vain.

" That is all lies," he fumed. " Let her come back, I shall murder her, I intend cutting her up in little pieces, please order her to return at once."

" I think I shall have to tell her to stay away if you feel like that," I remarked.

" No, Madam, she must come; she *must* come."

" If you hate her so why do you not follow your custom and marry another woman and let Kaironesa go ? "

" I will. But I'll murder her first."

" Then I think I cannot advise her to come back quickly."

" Then I'll go and murder her there."

" Really, you are rather bloodthirsty, aren't you ? A poor *gosha* woman."

" Oh, she is not a woman and *gosha*, she is a *male* woman," he hissed.

My poor Kaironesa, life is manifestly not all roses for

her! And she is a singularly refined and dignified woman. But when the taste of Roshan Saib's brutality was bitter in my mouth a visitor arrived who made me feel that India in some ways is able to teach us much.

Muni Sami, a Process Server from the District *Munsif's* Court called. India at its best, its sincerest, its most spiritual, is illustrated in him. Of ordinary primary education, his post but little above that of a court servant, his caste of the Sudra middle class, this man in his soul, in his spirit, towers above us everyday folks. For his passionate search after the highest puts us all to shame. It is his thought day and night. As he fares forth on the errands of the court a well-worn copy of *The Practice of Yoga* is unfailingly in his pocket and studied at every leisure moment. The *Bhagavat Gita* is also one of his treasures and, of recent years, the New Testament. "It agrees with all I think," he remarked at first with wonder, "there is nothing in it strange or contrary to our own spiritual ideals and knowledge."

But though he did not seem conscious of a direct new influence I think it was the central Figure in the Gospels which affected him most. He is very fond of reading the lives of old *yogis*, but it would hardly be *yogis* who spurred him on to practical actions. On his frequent tours he began to teach and preach. This news came from others; but, taxed with it, he admitted being known as a teacher on both spiritual and practical matters. The drink evil was one he set himself to combat. In one village a *Reddi* had become a wretched drunkard. The home was ruined, the man's wife had left him in despair. Muni Sami took him in hand. I do not know all he did and said; but the *Reddi* was helped to reform. He declared he owed his reclamation from drunkenness to Muni Sami. My friend Helen Powell went to see this *Reddi* and found him surrounded with the sick folk of the village to whom he attended daily, giving herb medicine to all and milk to those who were poor and needed it. The wife had returned, and the peace of the home was restored.

In order to follow the way of *yoga* more completely, to control the lower nature and increase spiritual power, Muni Sami has of recent years eschewed ordinary food. Milk and fruit, and the water the rice is boiled in for his family, are his only articles of diet. Yet he fulfils the duties of his post, which are often strenuous. Moreover, he is possessed of unusual common sense and practical ability. When a tour to North India was planned by a friend he rapidly worked out railway connections, fares and time-tables. But unfailingly one is conscious in him of the detached, God-absorbed spirit of the *yogi.* If ever there was a man of single purpose and with a single eye, seeking ceaselessly for the holy grail of God-nearness and God-likeness, and subordinating all daily life to this one great spiritual passion, it is Muni Sami of Penuroy. When I reach the many mansions may I be allowed to see him and the many spirit treasures he will have accumulated, for even now I feel this man is what Christ must have meant when he spoke of being "rich toward God."

If such as Muni Sami made up India, or even a good part of it, we should be moving steadily towards the millennium in this country. But this type is as rare here as at home.

Recently an educated Indian got into the railway carriage in which I was travelling. With the usual Indian readiness to be friendly if one holds out but a finger, he soon informed me he was the Government Registrar for Co-operative Societies in this district and several others.

"Are they flourishing?" I asked. "How do they prosper in the villages?"

"They ought to prosper," he replied, "for every *ryot* [1] wants to borrow and the usurer is the curse of the country; moreover the peasants can give us the security of their

[1] Peasant.

land. But our constant difficulty is that we cannot find reliable people to handle funds and affairs in the villages."

"But there are always at least one or two educated men in most villages, surely?" I asked.

"Can one trust them?" he said with disgust. "I am a Brahmin myself—but the Brahmins are the worst of all, untrustworthy scoundrels most of them!" And then followed a recital of cases in which village Co-operative Societies had been cheated out of their funds by rascally Brahmins.

"Perhaps what is wanted in this country is a little more Christianity?" I ventured.

"I am a Hindu," he replied, "and may have different views on that subject." His manner had grown a little more stiff and his flow of talk was arrested for the moment. Presently he came to from his reverie. "I must admit we need the Christian standards. I admit we need them desperately. I am a Christian College man myself, and I confess it has altered my standards for my whole life. There is this about Christianity, it is so plain—it teaches something to simple people. A little while ago I had to do with coolies. I had to classify them, so I asked each of what religion he was. One coolie woman said she was a Christian, and I asked her what she meant by that. I confess I asked just to make fun of her, for I saw she was quite uneducated and poor. To my surprise she answered at once, 'We must not steal, we must not tell lies, we must be kind, we must serve God.' She had some idea, she knew something! If I asked a Hindu coolie woman what she meant by being a Hindu she would not be able to say anything. Yes, we need the Christian standards! The absence of them makes the work of Co-operative Societies in the villages most difficult."

* * * * *

A patriotic meeting was arranged here in the Town Hall, to celebrate "Our Day," and to raise funds for comforts for the wounded. Waiting for it to begin I chatted with an ex-municipal chairman.

"I hope you have come equipped with many ideas how to celebrate?" I asked.

"No ideas at all," said the ex-chairman; "we leave that to you Europeans."

"Oh, but," I remonstrated, "with all this talk of Home Rule, don't you think you might contribute ideas?"

"No, we don't want ideas," he said, "all we want is the power of the purse. The power of the purse. Not ideas."

"But do you think, then, that money by itself confers the power of ruling? Don't you think that behind handling money must lie some thinking. . . . ?"

"No, no," he interrupted, "we don't want thought. Just the purse, the power of the purse, that is all we want."

These things make one think. Is there possibly at present something missing in the Indian make-up? Something that is essential to the power of governing? In another meeting later on, the Collector, himself a Brahmin, upbraided other members roundly for evincing self-interest. "Public spirit? You have not a grain of it!" he shouted frankly, and added other home truths which no European would have ventured to utter.

In private one may meet the same admissions. "We were better off under the British bureaucracy," said the president of a Board to me, "our people are not really fit to govern. I confess I am not myself. If they made me Collector to-morrow I know I could not fill the office. We cannot get rid of partisanship."

If this were a true diagnosis would the case be hopeless?

It is true that a triple tyranny is operative in India, with all its baneful and far-reaching results: the tyranny of caste over each of its members, forbidding a man to follow his convictions, his higher visions, his better sense, should they happen to contravene caste obligations; the tyranny of one sex over another; the tyranny of high caste over low, holding enthralled a sixth part of the whole population in conditions of slavery.

What will alter a national psychology inevitably affected by such conditions?

When I was last in Bukkuru I heard a story about my friend Rangavachari, who is President now of the Taluk Board. In that capacity he is responsible for all Board schools. He was on a tour of inspection. In Siddapur, where there is a Board school and also a private one, the *Panchamas*[1] came to him with a petition.

"Sir, we want our children to be educated."

"Very well, send them to the Board school," the president replied.

"But they are refused admittance there," the low caste people informed him. The president sent for the headmaster, a Brahmin.

"I understand some *Panchama* children here want to come to the Board school," Rangavachari said to him, "would you admit them?"

"No, sir, certainly not; never will I let the school be defiled," said the misguided headmaster, expecting approval of this Hindu righteousness.

"You definitely refuse to admit *Panchamas*?" asked the president again.

"Certainly, sir, I will never allow defilement in a Board school," replied the headmaster, convinced he was upholding principle to an admiring audience.

"Thank you, I will see you again later," the president told him.

The teacher of the private school was sent for. "Would you admit *Panchama* children in your school if they wanted to come?"

[1] Outcastes.

" Poor things, if they wanted to come, yes. It would be right to help them on."

The Brahmin was asked to return and bring all registers and records. Dumbfounded, he heard the pronouncement.

" You are herewith relieved from your post, as you are not willing to accept Government orders connected with that post. Government orders are that all schools supported by public money are open to all classes. The private school teacher is herewith appointed headmaster, the two schools will be amalgamated."

My informant chuckled as he told his tale. " There is a splendid school in Siddapur now and the *Panchamas* come! "

Here is justice and the capacity to govern fairly. But can it be said it developed in a purely Hindu atmosphere? Many years ago this man threw off the tyrannous yoke of caste and incurred great obloquy in consequence.[1]

" I am going to present a Bible to the reading-room of this town," he wrote to me recently. " Will you order for me a suitable copy? "

It is difficult to avoid the conviction that the element needed to free India from her age-long tyrannies, and to develop the fibre necessary for self-government, is the Christian element

[1] See *A Struggle for a Soul*, pp. 179 ff.

CHAPTER XVIII

"*AMMA*, a pencil, please."

"Please give me some paper to cover my book."

"I have nothing to put over me at night."

"The *dhobi* has my other skirt"—this to wrathful remarks of mine about the present very inky one.

Now I have become the old woman who lived in a shoe. The pitter-patter of little feet in the verandah, the chattering like magpies in the garden where ostensibly they are weeding, but in reality climbing the rapidly growing flame-trees, is like music in my ears. For is it not the fulfilment of the dream of years?

Dorcas is acting as matron. Her business capacities are finding fine scope. For to the multifarious other duties of the missionary it was impossible to add the daily supervision of housekeeping details in the Home. Dorcas and I settled principles. First, children must have nourishing food and plenty of it, also variety, else they will think unduly much about food. Second, economy is essential. Third, responsibility for, and the credit of doing it all as well as possible, rests with the matron. The result appears to be, so far, that the cost per head is lower than elsewhere and that not a single complaint about food has reached us.

The question of discipline came up next and proved a thorny subject. In how far are punishments ever truly salutary? When life opens and coercive preventives are withdrawn what inner bulwarks have they built? I can see that the building up of these is going to be a slow business. A few days ago we played the ring game. Between these Christian village children and their little heathen neighbours there is not much perceptible difference. While

I was hiding the ring I saw the girls peeping and peering. A teacher had to be put in charge to prevent them cheating. Then, quite openly, they tugged at the teacher's skirt. "Tell us where it is. Tell us just this time."

"Shall we play the ring game?" I asked to-day.

"Oh, yes, yes, please."

I drew it from my finger and in front of them stuffed it into some hiding-place.

"Now find it."

They gazed at me in perplexity. "But we saw where you put it."

"The other day I noticed you looking when I hid it; so I thought you liked it this way."

"But—but, that's not a game!"

"No, it is not a game. Do you really want to play a game?"

"Oh yes, yes."

"Then, *play the game*!"

But it will take time to get the notion of honour rooted among them. Though even now, I overhear little whispers, "We must play the game; we must not look."

* * * * *

The question of punishments has been solved not unsatisfactorily, I hope. The matron has a mark book. Three bad marks—which, however, are not to be lightly given, and only for direct disobedience or very gross negligence—involve the loss of the Sunday rosette. This is a pink affair, solemnly pinned on when they are marched up in their white Sunday things for inspection before service. The loss of it is a punishment purely of the imagination; but the sensitiveness appealed to has not failed. They mind it badly and have besought me even with tears to relax my hardness of heart, which, needless to state, is inexorable.

Maybe, in part, their grief is feminine vanity. Certainly the spectacle of the little crocodile of snow-white girls with their rosettes is so fetching that I now get visits from tiny Andapur mites. Two of them stood in the verandah yesterday and asked solemnly, " Please take *us* into the Home. We want a pink flower."

Quarrelling is another difficulty. This does not trouble me personally anything like as much as the lack of truth, or tendency to laziness. Sneakingly I even sympathize with the children. Who expects them to have the tempers of angels; boys may fight it out; girls must somehow express their instinct of combativeness also. The matron, however, likes things more orderly; she caused me to harangue them, and make them understand that this pastime must be kept within bounds, or their liberty may be curtailed. In spite of this (Dorcas has just been in to say), two of the bigger girls had quarrelled disgracefully in school and on the way home. This last is particularly heinous. On public roads! The rosette will not cover the crime, matron thought. There is to be a picnic next week; exclusion from that might serve. Is not that rather too fearful ? Also, who would look after them, left behind all day alone ? With a sigh, I sent for the culprits and groped for wisdom. They stood before me with heads hanging low.

" Long ago, before people had any houses, where did they live ? " I began.

The heads went up. Instead of a scolding, something like a story. Things were not so awful, apparently.

" Yes, in the jungle. Is anyone living in the jungle now ? No ? Think again. Yes, tigers and other animals. But human beings learned to build houses. Living together in numbers they had to make rules for themselves, had they not ? Is there a *Panchayat* [1] in your village ? Quite so, and every one has to obey it. If they won't obey it, the others will have

[1] Village council of five elders.

nothing to do with them, they must go away to the jungle. And, in the same way. . . ."

Heads went down again. This story had a horrid moral after all.

"I am sorry; but if you will behave like jungle animals you must be in 'the jungle.' For this week you will not eat with the others, but have your food out in the courtyard by yourselves."

They departed, impressed, I trust, with a sense of disgrace. Their imagination must surely be getting a little trained; for in itself the punishment is fictitious. A short time ago, on full moon night, every one had their food out in the playground and that "jungle" was *pro tem.* the abode of bliss.

* * * * *

This evening I went round to the Home at dusk as usual. Just at present we are striving to learn taking our part in the Sunday service. The Ten Commandments have been mastered by all. They were to learn the Confession of Sins.

They had not learned anything. "We had no book." I thought we would start learning it now, but found to my dismay that for the life of me I could not remember how it began in Telugu. Between the young who had not learnt and the old who had forgotten, there did not seem much to choose, so I freely forgave us all and thought we might turn to a fairy story instead.

"But tell us the same one you told us last Saturday." Saturday is the day reserved for such things.

"Which was that?"

"Sleeping Girl!" "Thorn Flower!"—called various voices, and a hot discussion ensued till we had decided on a name for "Sleeping Beauty."

"A-hundred-years-sleeping-girl," we settled on in the

end, not as cumbersome in Telugu as in English, and also, I foresee, useful as nickname for not improbable occasions!

Afterwards we sat on the steps outside and gazed at the stars. Perhaps I expected too much of the children, yet in this country of wonderful starlit nights and constant open-air life I was surprised that none of them had observed that (according to our usual parlance) stars rise and set. As we watched to-night the heavenly bodies became very interesting in their performances. Also I became conscious of many a hiatus in my astronomy and shall have to furbish up!

"Please will you give me a *bottu* for sweets?" said a confiding voice at my window this morning. "My father said he would send, but he did not, and I want some so very much."

"And the walls were all made of gingerbread and the windows of candy sugar. . . ." I fear we shall have to eliminate *that* fairy story from our *repertoire.* Evidently I am leading their innocent youth astray. The other children were superiorly horrified at the petitioner's boldness and badness, and indeed she did not get her *bottu*, an act of odious self-denial on my part.

I am glad they have ceased to regard me as an object of reverence, if not terror. At first they did. A little newcomer had inflamed eyelids, I took her to hospital to have the eyes washed out—an unpleasing job and she would not keep still. "Be brave; don't move," I exhorted her. She bore it without flinching. Next morning I let the school conductress go with the patient. They returned after an hour. I looked at the eyes.

"But they have not been washed to-day?"

"No, she would not keep still."

"Back you go and have them washed. I am coming to see it done."

But delay occurred on the way. I perceived one of my Hindu schoolgirls sitting outside her house. " Why are you not at school ? " I called in passing.

" Scorpion sting."

I jumped off the cycle and looked at her foot; it had happened a day or two before; they had put some concoction on and the foot was swollen and seemed to be going septic. " It must be disinfected, why don't you take her to hospital ? " I asked the mother.

" She cannot walk there, she is too big to be carried, we have no money for a cart."

" You'll come on my cycle ? " To the glee of all the juveniles in the neighbourhood who followed us in shoals, I wheeled her to hospital and had her attended to. When I looked for my own refractory lamb she could not be found anywhere. Inquired of, the authorities said, " She was here; she let us do everything, she said you were coming."

Being an ogre has its uses.

They have been so good now for a week or two that it is uncanny. There surely ought to be some naughtiness about ? I live in hope.

Mr. Rangavachari came to see me yesterday. He was to address a students' meeting and invited me to come. The hall was packed with students, and the platform with the Andapur *élite*. The annual report was followed by a " prayer," i.e. a lyric sung by a student and applauded by the audience. Rangavachari's address was splendid. He ignored the platform and spoke straight to the students. His points were these. (1) Consider your minds a garden; sow good seeds and banish weeds. (2) Endeavour every day to write down a good and helpful thought. (3) Cultivate a sense of wonder. The universe is full of revelations; search for and observe them reverently. Here followed natural history illustrations. (4) Have a hobby. Never become a mere bookworm, or a place hunter. (5) Let all study lead to service of others. That is success in life, not a career, but ability to help others.

"You gave us almost a Christian sermon," I said as we walked back.

"I am proud you call it that," he replied, "but it is not exclusively Christian."

"I noticed," I persisted, "that all your quotations were modern, and except for a single one from Rabindranath Tagore, drawn from English authors. You supported your words almost entirely from English, not Hindu minds."

"Didn't I admit this morning," he said, "how much we owed to England and English ideas?"

"English ideas—Christian ideas," I meditated.

"Yes, Christian," he admitted. "That reminds me of a recent happening in our Widows' Home. We invited a destitute caste woman with her three daughters there. 'It is not a Christian place?' she asked. 'No, no,' I told her, 'it is altogether Hindu.' 'I want to see it first,' she stipulated. She came and went over the premises. What do you think she said? 'I cannot stay, I don't want to lose my caste; I should lose it if I stayed in a Christian place like this.' Nothing would persuade her it was Hindu; she went away. You have visited it. I ask you, what is there that is Christian?"

I laughed. "The whole spirit of it. The woman's instinct was quite right. She recognized something not produced by Hinduism. She saw the likeness to Christian institutions. It breathes out Christianity, not Hinduism. If you *will* act like a Christian what can you expect? And how very generous of you to give your case away by this story!"

It was nearly nine o'clock when I got home and next day the children were pathetic. "We did the weeding in the garden, truly, all; we wanted to show you. We sat on the steps and waited and waited. The dogs barked in the next compound, we said, 'Here she comes.' But no one came and we waited. We thought 'Now she would be telling us lovely stories, she would be teaching us nice songs,' we asked where you were and no one knew where you had gone. We did not know what had happened, and it grew darker and darker and so we went home at last."

Bless them. I must not rush off to students' meetings without accounting to them first, must I ?

There is a new girl, a relative of Radha's, and small as she is I can feel her influence already telling for good. No cheating with little Jewel. Then two sisters have come, daughters of a good mother, and here too, I feel the difference in character. Fat little Margaret and Jewel are the smallest in the Home, and it taxes my ingenuity to hide my preference.

All of us are mad on gardening. It is a struggle here! like everything else. I sowed balsam seeds and they came up in hundreds; when an inch high they sank down and died as if cut by a scythe. Hurriedly I took out the poor remaining few and came upon a horrid insect in the seed pan, a spider which I killed with venomous gusto. The carefully planted out cosmos were eaten by grasshoppers, and the little beasts snap their metaphorical fingers at me, for I don't know how to get at them. Hares came in and devoured the sunflowers, but I am up to the hares. The space under the wire netting where they squeezed in has been filled up. Dealing with earth inspired me further to make garden seats—mud heaps with slabs over them; great was the joy of the children over these.

"This is *my* place!" came a shout over the newly discovered seat, "I am the garden watchman. Here I sleep," and she flung herself down on it in true Indian watchman fashion. "No, *my* place," cried another; "here I beat the dry manure into powder." This is one of their jobs—collecting the cattle manure from all over the compound, laying it out to dry, then powdering it into "flour" as they call it. " A fat lot you will beat," said another, " look at the heap *I* have collected! " " I want to see the Jesus thorn," said another, running up to me. (This is a cactus with a tiny red blossom.) " Couldn't we," interrupted my pet Margaret, " couldn't we bring up a little baby ? " In her own home there are so many, perhaps she missed them. I told her that bringing up the lot of *them* was sufficient work for me for the present. " But it would be nice to have a baby," persisted Margaret. " *We* would look after it."

" Look, three presents for me to-day! " called Siromani. Everybody promptly left off working and ran to look at the wonders. A bit of lead—the internal economy of a perished pencil—a button, a bead. These have been found in the quest for manure.

" Do you know what is over there ? " asked Jivi, and from the awe of her tone I inferred at least an aeroplane; but the keenest of glances directed over there discovered nothing worth notice.

" A sieve," she explained to my opaque vision.

" Fetch it," I commanded. Sieves are precious. She returned and presented a bit of perforated zinc, the decrepit panel of an old meat-safe, reposing there in its dotage.

" You may have it," I said.

She looked at me rapturously, overpowered by this unbelievable generosity on my part, and started sifting with this new toy. She obtained such lovely fine earth that I was inspired to try it forthwith for sowing petunia seeds, while Jivi stuttered with pride.

A basket of plants arrived to-day for the garden. It galvanized us all into our utmost, even the waterman. Generally his formulæ for avoiding work show true inventiveness. " Who can work in the rain ? " when it is drizzling; " who can work in the sun ? " if the weather is fine; " who can work so late ? " if it is neither wet nor hot, just getting nice and cool. But to-day he worked with a will

—I hope the new plants feel conscious of welcome. The children rushed to gaze at the latest wonders. "What is that?" "What is this?" they asked, demanding names.

Of one bush I only knew the botanical name; but it saves trouble to answer the children. "That is a *Lagerstrœmia*," I replied. They laughed, or looked perplexed at the odd sounds, but a little voice behind me repeated with exquisite clearness, "*Lagerstrœmia*." Margaret, of course; she has the quickest ear and the most flexible tongue! To hear her say her verses, every syllable given its full value, is an æsthetic pleasure after the slovenly pronunciation of most village children.

I need not have worried about the girls being too immaculate. No less than seven lost their rosettes on Sunday. Four for being "not clean." Inwardly I pitied them, for this is really the fault of the parents, not training them in nice ways early. Let us hope the discipline will impress the girls sufficiently to train *their* children! Two had quarrelled and one had told a lie. This was silly Eunice, aged sixteen, who always says what occurs to her, a lie as readily as anything, a girl with no grit and no depth, foolish and amiable. Eunice has come to the Home too late—I begin to feel like Margaret, and want to bring them up from babyhood. Considering the moral as well as economic depression most of our Christians are reared in this would not be a bad plan, if we would have better parents later on. Only what about being the old woman in the shoe *then*?

Last Sunday the Creation was their lesson, I took them out into the garden; we had seeds and flowers and leaves to help us along. In details the children are singularly unobservant and unused to loving nature. A flower is something to stick in their hair; that is the *alpha* and *omega* of it. From "thoughts too deep for tears" they are yet a long way off. Still they love them; on this foundation may be built much.

* * * * *

The oleanders are in deep bloom; I was collecting big double blossoms early this morning for the children. Those who have a rosette may have a flower also. If it feeds vanity let us hope it also educates their sense of beauty. It satisfies mine! The rows of white figures, pink rosette on shoulder, in each black hair-knot a red flower is a sight pleasing, not only to me, but surely also to the Maker of children and of flowers.

Meditating happily on this as I was gathering blossoms I saw the matron come tearing along. Trouble had occurred in the Home, the unmistakable evidence of misbehaviour was there, no girl would own to it. And it was nearly time to go to church; some girl was lying, what about flowers and rosettes? "Send them all here," I said in perplexity, and did my frequent groping after wisdom.

Presently they stood before me uncomfortable and unhappy. "This has occurred. We do not want it to spoil God's day of joy for all of us. This once, the child that has done it shall be forgiven. But she must confess. You will come in, one by one, and the child that has done it will tell me. I shall not tell anyone. Let us begin with the smallest."

That was Margaret. She came in. Her face is round and grave, she looked at me with serious eyes. "Did you do it, Margaret?" I asked. In reality I suspected two others who came from a motherless home and an unreliable father. To my surprise Margaret burst out sobbing, "Yes, I did!"

"Why did you say you did not?"

"They would *all* laugh at me; they would all scold me, I could not bear it."

Poor little over-burdened child heart. Public exposure is a fearful penalty; are we not expecting a courage beyond their powers in asking them to face it? The punishment other children inflict in self-righteousness is too heavy a burden.

To keep my word and shield her the others had each to be asked; nearly we were late for church! But we all went with a lighter heart for the announcement that confession had been made and sins were forgiven and every one might wear flowers!

* * * * *

All of them have been organized into little Committees for the self-government of the Home. "Helpers" have to be pioneers in volunteering for odd jobs, "Comforters" take charge of new-comers and shy and small girls, "House cleanliness" is responsible for every nook and corner inside being clean, "Golden mouth" is to see that no bad words are used or any slovenly or unsuitable talk going on, "Peace-makers" must suppress incipient quarrels, "Early birds" assist the matron in the early rising of every one (a great battle in the Home), "Remembrance" has to keep every one to their tasks—that is, if anything is amiss, find out who is in charge of it and keep them to it.

Slowly, slowly, I hope we are making our way towards establishing that mysterious something called "a good tone" in our Home. When once that is there the place will, so to speak, run itself.

The first requisite for this I consider to be happiness. Unhappy children, frequently punished children, cannot produce it. The second is as important—and almost synonymous—liberty. Not hedged in by restrictions on every hand. Not having a time-table full from morning till night. The third is regular work within their powers, the fourth, a long way behind, is discipline. Not much of it, but where it exists, inexorable.

The most important is so self-evident that I have not mentioned it at all.

CHAPTER XIX

THREE days ago Jaiamma, our teacher, came with a piteous tale. Kona, a former schoolgirl here, had married a man of her caste, a barber. He turned out to be a terrible drunkard who beat her and otherwise made life unendurable for her. She ran back to her parents. When the visit lengthened beyond the time custom allowed, the parents, in spite of her tears and imploring, sent her back. " If you must die under his hand you must," they said. " We cannot go against custom."

Kona bore it for some time. The point beyond which she could not endure was reached again. (Being young it is possible her powers of endurance were not well developed yet.) The parental home being precluded she found work as servant in a Brahmin house. There she was seen by *Bogum*[1] women who persuaded her to come to their house. Whether they had represented things to her falsely is not known; after a few days she effected her escape from them and made for Andapur, where, utterly desperate, she again implored shelter. The door was closed against her. " You have broken our caste, you cannot enter," was the parents' welcome to their prodigal.

The sun was sinking; shelterless, foodless, she stood in the streets of Andapur. Where to go ? The thought of her old school came as a ray of hope. Alas! she found it locked up; teachers and pupils had gone home for the day. But her old teacher's house was found. Jaiamma kept her for the night and brought her to me next day.

Here was a problem. A married Hindu girl, cast out by parents, her married home impossible; one who has been in prostitutes' houses—what could be done ? There she stood and fell at my feet. " Let me come into the Home."

[1] See p. 29.

But mixing up a Boarding School and Rescue Home work is no more feasible in India than in England; to have daughters of Christian parents and young married Hindu women of possibly doubtful antecedents in our Home would risk its whole atmosphere. Then are we to send Kona simply adrift ? Long I pondered.

" Dorcas, let us go to the parents and beg them to take in their child."

The father and mother looked such kindly people that my hopes rose high. When we started our interceding the mother began to weep bitterly. The father, too, looked sorrowful; there was no trace of anger in either parent, only affection and sadness. Nevertheless they were adamant.

" Not into this house, not even into this street may she set foot. Not since she has taken the *Bogum* people's food."

That was the real crime. Not immorality in itself, that might be condoned—but taking the food of another caste could not be forgiven.

It was a strange scene in that little room; the mother almost speechless from weeping, the father scarcely spoke for sorrow; they evidently longed to follow the dictates of love and pity, but cruelly caste stood in the way. We, the representatives of another faith, besought them in vain to obey the true laws of religion.

" Why do *you* not take her ? " said the mother at last. " You Christian people take everybody. To us she must be dead. But if you looked after her we should be glad."

To the Boarding Home, straight from the *Bogums*, is an impossible path. Can the girl be persuaded to go to a Rescue Home in Mysore ?

But Hinduism kept watchful eyes. From Jaiamma's house the girl was decoyed away. The *Bogum* people had her again. Dorcas hunted the town high and low; inquiries elicited but the rumour that she had been spirited away to another town; we could not pretend to the position of legal guardians, and invoke the aid of authorities. Caste can punish and cast out; but can it protect and help in desperate need?

* * * * *

Six weeks passed, then she turned up frightened, hurried, at Jaiamma's house one evening, having again made her escape from the *Bogums*. "But I cannot go to strange people, I will only stay with you or Missiamma."

Problems are raining upon me. Hardly was this interview over when a cart drove up. It was Kaironesa. It is some time since her return after her sister's death from plague. She had brought with her the sister's motherless little son; I hoped in the childless home this would make for peace. But she had also brought some jewels belonging to relatives which, with her own, she kept hidden. Her husband had discovered the hoard and appropriated all. The relatives went to court on the matter. On entering the room she flung herself at my feet, entirely unstrung. "Now he will kill me," she gibbered. "You don't know him; he will murder me."

I remembered a former conversation and had fewer doubts than she credited me with.

"Come and live in this compound for a few days," I suggested. "He is not likely to perpetrate a crime here." In fear and trembling she consented.

Her terror was piteous. And she was, as a rule, so self-controlled and dignified a woman.

I had a report from one of our Christian families living near Kaironesa that one evening they had had to rush in, hearing her cries; they held on to the husband by main force to prevent her being injured or worse. He does not support her himself, yet objects to her finding independent work. She is to be with him, go in fear of her life and earn her own living too. I cannot discover that there is any legal protection; in any case for a *gosha* woman to go into court would make her feel disgraced. The wonder is that Mohammedan women have not turned suffragettes in a body long ago! But the " inferiority complex " has bitten deep.

This poor woman wants to stay here permanently; she would adopt the Christian religion, not from special conviction, but from desire of a quiet life. The change from the conditions of her home impressed her into exclaiming, " This is heaven! " The happy children with their laughter and games and busy tasks, the other teachers, kindly and helpful to the scared new-comer, everybody unafraid—all this, when contrasted with her own life full of terror and tyranny, must make this place seem heaven to her. No wonder she would like to stay; be a Christian, be anything, only live in this atmosphere of peace.

Alas! her days of happiness were numbered; though she did not obey messages to return the man found a way to compel her. He prowled round when most of us were out and saw the boy, her late sister's son, playing about, and called the child. The little chap, in deadly fear of him, dared not disobey; the man snatched him up and ran. His game was won. Kaironesa had to go when he took the child. " What shall I do ? What shall I do ? " she kept on repeating, in a dazed way. I had a last talk with her and told her to remember she had friends here always. It was hard to let her go, with no protection, no love, no intimacy anywhere; but as things were I had no choice.

*   *   *   *

My troubles with this man Roshan Saib are by no means over. True, I feel a little comforted about Kaironesa, for she wrote that she and the boy are in Secundarabad with relatives, and that she has found a post in a Government school there. But the man still comes to these parts on his optician's business. I am writing from Bukkuru. What was my dismay to find among the Mohammedan houses here

Zakina Bi, the orphaned girl whom Kaironesa brought up. "Why have you not gone with the *Bibi* ?" I asked.

A miserable story came out. Kaironesa was arranging a marriage for her. Meanwhile Roshan Saib had made improper overtures to the girl who was practically their adopted daughter. "You are not to agree to this marriage proposal," he threatened her. "If you do I will kill you." Terrified of him, Zakina refused the marriage. Kaironesa, guessing future trouble, but ignorant of the fact that it was already upon them, put an ultimatum, "Agree to the marriage, or I cannot take you with me." The husband, terrorizing Zakina in secret, prevailed upon the girl to choose the alternative of being left behind.

So here she is now in Bukkuru in a house rented by Roshan Saib; he comes occasionally on his business rounds and finds a private establishment a convenience. Her good name is gone; the man does not send enough money for her maintenance. She is lonely and unhappy and cannot bear the loss of her self-respect. Neighbours looked askance at her. With tears she flung herself upon me when she saw me.

"Let me be with you! I have no one in the world. My people were all drowned in the Hyderabad floods; the *Bibi* took me, but now she will not have me, I cannot bear it here, no honour, no friend—let me come to the Christians, I have no one at all."

What is one to do with an appeal like that? She is not actuated in the least by any desire for Christian teaching, only conscious of bitter need of help. How much we need a Home for such women! It might be a united one for several Missions. Alack! it always means funds. The private purse of a missionary is not long; Committee funds are parcelled out with scrupulous exactitude, leaving no margin; appeal for private subscriptions is forbidden. What then is one to do in the face of a need like this?

The financial difficulty, real as it was, shrank into nothing before others. This terrible man, roused to fury, what would he do? And the Mohammedans in general, though they looked on calmly and callously at the ruin of a girl by one of themselves, would unite as one man against her seeking the protection of another faith.

"I cannot promise to take you," I said perplexedly. "You should have held on to the *Bibi.* She was your true benefactress; you owed her confidence and support."

But every evening, when I returned in the dark from the day's work in schools and houses, there stood Zakina, hiding behind a pillar. "You must not leave me here, indeed you must not leave me here alone," she reiterated piteously. She wore down my reason, my awe of Committees, my worldly considerations for the rest of our Mohammedan work, till nothing but a little Christianity was left. "Then come with me," I said resignedly at last, wondering what it would mean. That Roshan Saib is always up and down our railway line; I doubt if I could safely get the girl anywhere without his knowledge, he would manage to abduct her *en route* somehow. Though the decision was only arrived at this evening and to-morrow morning is the time for departure, I should not wonder if he knows all about it already! He has the most uncanny *flair* for discovering things.

Andapur. On the journey here Zakina was in my carriage in the train. At the various stations she hid under the seat. At Dharmpalli Junction I had unpacked my tiffin basket and was about to begin supper. A face appeared at the window. It was Roshan Saib! I sat petrified. I had hoped he was in Hyderabad or, preferably, if wishes could take him there, the middle of the Sahara—but no. He was here looking in at my window The devil must inspire him!

"You come from Bukkuru?" asked this omniscient villain. "You have seen Zakina?"

My wits had entirely congealed. For lying I possessed

no handy facilities. Zakina, squirming under the seat, froze all power of counter-questions, or evasions. I simply sat dumb with fright, all my being concentrated on the one coherent wish that he would go away.

A little astonished at my failure to respond to polite greetings he looked again into the carriage and saw my supper preparations. Ah, that explained it; the Miss Sahiba was having her meal! The privacy of meals is sacred in India. He apologized and withdrew.

Saved for the moment! But not for long.

He came round to the Mission compound the next afternoon. " You have that girl."

" Yes," I admitted.

" I want her," he snorted.

" By all means, if she will go. Let her do as she likes," I replied.

" Please send for her."

" I will, but can you call at 5.30 ? I have urgent letters to get ready for the post first." It was then about 4.30.

" I will wait." The accumulated office work was attacked and letters despatched. Also a note was hastily sent to the Police Inspector requesting his immediate presence. There was no knowing what violence might be attempted.

Very obligingly he came at once. At sight of him the Saib vanished. I discussed the case with the Inspector; he advised having a *Panchayat* and letting the girl declare her intention before them—a very good suggestion.

Nervousness and fear began to invade this peaceful compound. Dorcas came to say the man was prowling round the Mohammedan school; that he had got three girls away and tried to trouble the teacher; and in a general way was breathing out threatenings and slaughter. Several Mohammedan women arrived, sent up by Roshan; they demanded speech with Zakina and tried their best to persuade her to go back with them.

A friendly Hindu woman came and warned me of the Saib's threats in the bazaar, also that he had the station watched, and probably most stations along the line. Zakina by this time was so frightened that she declared she would go to him sooner than make all this trouble and enrage him further. But he would certainly vent his rage on her; and in any case, what is her future? When he tires of her, as she is alone in the world, nothing but the streets. The Council of Arbitration was arranged. I told her to hold on to courage and declare she wished to stay here.

Meanwhile the Mohammedan school was absolutely empty; the rumour having spread all over the town that I had abducted a Mohammedan girl and was keeping her forcibly imprisoned in the Mission compound, intending, no doubt, also forcibly, to baptize her. The very situation I foresaw and feared. If Zakina elects to stay it will be accentuated; if her courage fails and she goes, what will be her fate? No outlook is very promising. What would one do in such hours but for the consciousness that "the angel of the Lord who encompasseth round about them that fear Him" has a longer vision than ours and commands powers exceeding those of the enemy?

"Heavenly Guardian of Zakina, and of the Mission work here, please find a way out when we see none!"

The *Panchayat* assembled. Roshan demanded private speech with Zakina. It was refused. Let him speak plainly before all.

"Come to my house," he said to the girl.

"I will not come to your house," the girl whispered, hanging her head.

Roshan looked nonplussed. "But I will marry you," he offered. "Only come."

Zakina lifted her head. "If it is a marriage before the *Khazi* I will come."

The way out! There was still endless disputing; Roshan

was bent on taking her away at once; still intending, I feared, to slither out of the marriage; but the *Panchayat* decreed she should stay under the protection of the Mission till the ceremony was arranged; a matter apparently of only a few hours.

Now every one is happy! The Mohammedan teacher looked radiant when she heard of it. "You are getting her properly married; that *is* a meritorious work, now all is well." The man is pleased at getting her away from me, convinced I meant to steal her; the girl is pleased because she will be respectably married; I, because she is saved from the wretched state of easily discarded mistress; our Christians, because our school here is no longer jeopardized on account of my "stealing people." The one person not pleased will be my dear Kaironesa; to have her adopted daughter now as a co-wife will be trying; but it is not likely they will ever be in the same town.

The *palaver* was still going on in the verandah when the noise of drums and tomtoms resounded in the compound—another party bent on betrothal was arriving. There were certain similar features between the two brides-elect. Both were outwardly very plain and unattractive girls; Rose, the young Christian teacher, has only one eye and is generally very insignificant looking. Zakina is pock-marked and has a bad squint. Both are orphaned and without relatives; both come from a lowly estate, neither of them has much grit and character; both, but for the befriending of the Mission, would in all probability have gone to the bad. There the likeness ends. The Mohammedan woman was asked and taken in an interview without honour, or love; instead of gifts the persons concerned came near to a flaring quarrel in the middle of the betrothal over money matters. The Christian girl's ceremony was honoured by the presence of half our congregation; hymns were sung and prayer offered, jewels bestowed and *tambulam* distributed amid general rejoicing; it was a scene of festive gladness, the heroine of it all this one-eyed *Mala* girl. The two scenes happening within the same hour seemed to me a tangible illustration of the value and the dignity Christianity sets upon woman, while Mohammedanism tramples on her and holds her lightly.

* * * * *

Zakina was duly married before the *Khazi*. I witnessed the performance, and may I never see a more desolate wedding. Picture a tiny room, dark and windowless, divided by a curtain; on one side of it sat Zakina alone, wearing the same soiled and common garments she had travelled in from Bukkuru; on the other, with difficulty, three men found room, the *Khazi*, the bridegroom, and the bride's "advocate," who made all the responses on her behalf when the *Khazi* read the "service." I stood at the end of the curtain; one foot on the girl's side, one on the men's, and watched a ceremony which, again, seemed painfully to illustrate what Islam thinks of woman; there was not a single thing for the bride to do or say, she sat there invisible, inaudible; evidently it is her silence that implies consent. Hindu weddings give a very different importance to the woman.

Zakina is now installed in a hut in the bazaar; the man is off on his commercial travels. She sent a request to be permitted to come to the school and go on with her reading. Needless to say it was gladly allowed.

* * * * *

Some months later. Little did I dream for what reason the request was made. We of the West will always be at the mercy of the East, it seems to me, because of our foolish unsuspiciousness. Should the East be disposed to lead us by the nose it will find no difficulty. In the school Fatima Bi is teaching, a singularly dignified, reserved, and proud woman; one whom I had befriended for years and sent for training to a neighbouring Mission working among Mohammedans.

She is a widow and has some property. How Roshan Saib found this out is a mystery to me, his Secret Intelligence Department works to perfection. He cast an eye on her possessions, and used Zakina Bi to make overtures to her. The exchange of notes went on briskly. And now Fatima also has fallen to his bow and spear and married the man!

On my return from a week in camp Dorcas welcomed me with this continuation of the Mohammedan epic, also with the further news that its immediate consequence was the complete emptiness of the Mohammedan school. For all the parents feel affronted. " Is this what goes on in the school ? How could a widow with no relatives here arrange a marriage for herself ? Is she without shame, to interview a man ? Is the school a marriage-office ? " The Christian teacher had noticed nothing. It seemed natural that after school hours Zakina should stay behind to get extra coaching from Fatima.

But the incredible folly of Fatima! Her eldest daughter was betrothed to a student in the College here; he broke off the engagement immediately on hearing of Fatima's fatal step. Her son besought her not to marry this man, knowing his reputation; but she would, she would, she *would*! " The dangerous age," I imagine. Poor women—lines are laid for them in hard places.

Meanwhile it is my difficult job to soothe down the Mohammedans and pick up the school again. Old Ghulab Khan from Bukkuru has been sent for; he is too ancient to be of any use as a teacher, but he is esteemed by every one and will help the school to assemble its torn rags of respectability into a decent garment again.

* * * * *

With Fatima, naturally, the expected happened; within two weeks she was filled with remorse. Roshan had persuaded her to give her jewels into his care; having obtained these he neglected her. She has lost her post and salary, and her private possessions as well. A further legacy is a bad disease; she will have to go to Bangalore for treatment. Words fail me when I think of this Bluebeard, and of the religious system which permits a man of this kind to secure one deceived specimen of womanhood after another for his collection, plunging them into misery.

* * * * *

As if to add another touch to the picture of Moslem women, a letter arrived from Zainab Bi, my dear little friend and guest of two years ago. After leaving here she was baptized into the Christian faith, her husband consenting, but the rest of the family kept in ignorance of the fact.

"Dear Miss Sahiba, what shall I do?" she wrote. "Till my husband finds a post we have to live here with his father. My sister-in-law said yesterday, 'Does your daughter Tara not know any *kalmas*?'[1] Tara heard her and said, 'Yes, I know *kalmas*.' She began to sing loudly, 'Gentle Jesus meek and mild.' My sister-in-law does not know English and only said, 'Oh you have taught her *Feringi* songs.' Then my father-in-law came in. Tara ran to him, for he is always kind to her, and said, 'Shall I say *kalmas* to you?' He was pleased and said 'Yes.' Tara knelt down and began to say clearly, 'Our Father Who art in heaven.' When my father-in-law heard these words he pulled her up from her knees, and said with great anger, 'If you ever say that again I will beat you.' To me he said, 'It is that *shaitan*, your brother. If you follow his teaching it will be the worse for you. I will now see that you say *namaz* five times a day and Tara shall learn too.' What shall I do, Miss Sahiba? I cannot bear Tara being made into a little Mohammedan; but I have no liberty, no liberty at all."

What shall we do to get liberty for Zainab Bi?

I have written to reinforce in every possible way her own urgent desire that her husband take a separate house. Also, if anyhow it can be managed, to send Tara here.

[1] Prayers.

CHAPTER XX

Two little arrivals brought extra stir into our Home a few days ago. Both were the result of a long struggle. One is Shanti, whose mother had to be received in the Rescue Home in Mysore. From there she had sent us pathetic requests to take her child from the ignorant grandparents in the village and educate her in the Home. But the grandparents would not give her up. Letters had no effect and messengers returned empty-handed. At last a very energetic catechist was sent, with instructions to threaten the rigours of the law; for the mother is the legal guardian. He found the little thing in the cotton fields, earning wages for the selfish grandparents. He took her away and brought her as she was, a typical picture of a famine waif, arms and legs like sticks, stomach protruding from eating what she could find, hair clotted and filthy, and in a general way dirty beyond description; shy and frightened to boot, even of the other children at first. But Jewel, herself only seven, has a heart for the whole world. She welcomed the small derelict with open arms, unrepelled. God bless her little mother heart!

The other arrival looks like a princess in comparison—it is Tara! safely here after months of correspondence and effort. She is a bundle of mischief and every one's pet. She speaks Hindustani fluently, a fair amount of English, and scraps of Tamil; the only language the other girls know is Telugu. But Tara can take the tower of Babel in her stride! She has all the girls under her thumb; when she wishes to teach them anything the affair marches. I came into the moonlit playground yesterday and found a merry crowd dancing and singing in English "Ring a ring o' roses." Presently, under further instructions from Tara, they broke into "Oranges and Lemons." What is Tara's secret Esperanto? She is the smallest child in the Home; but apparently one has but to wish as she does that the girls should know something and do something, and promptly they know it and do it, and there you are!

Teaching must be the easiest profession in the world.

But our occasions are not always so lawful or joyous. Last Sunday a jubilant string of girls had been for a walk—a very depressed one followed me back on Monday. For when I went over to the Home to my utmost surprise I found no one there. Searching farther afield I found they had all gone "on the spree"; in the field beyond the compound they were—not to put too fine a point on it—stealing groundnuts. A tall and towering Missiamma came upon them. "Are these your ground nuts?"

"N-n-no."

"May you take other people's groundnuts?"

"N-n-no."

"Did the matron give you leave to go outside the compound?"

"N-n-no."

All spoils had to be dropped; a subdued group followed a silent missionary home. No further words were spoken, no punishment inflicted. But the light had gone out! Those that had duties went about them with great energy; those that had not I took with me to work in the garden, late as it was, and kept them at it in the moonlight, then sent them back. No story, no game, nothing nice, only one last stern word, "To-morrow the rest of this must be finished." Then we all went heavy hearted to our joyless suppers.

Into my sweet slumbers before the dawn stole the sound of whispers and footsteps. I arose from my bed in the verandah upstairs and peered into the garden. There, with scarcely light enough to see, were repentant girls weeding for dear life. A kindly twilight hid the smile on the face of the stern watcher above them.

Midday found me at my office table. Suddenly three little figures appeared in the doorway and without warning fell on their knees, " Please, please forgive us! "

I only wanted to hug them! Why was I born to uphold the majesty of law to anybody? This is terrible discipline for all concerned, but worse for me.

" Get up and come here." Presently they went away, subdued but free from a load. Within half an hour there was further whispering and pushing at the door. " Go in—you go first, kneel down, mind you each kneel. . . ." I went on steadfastly writing while they carried out their programme, behind my chair fortunately; thus giving me a chance to struggle for composure. Then the chorus at the back arose. " Please forgive us, we did not think; never will we do it again, only forgive us. . . ." I turned round to see uplifted tearful faces and raised folded hands—it seemed as if they were offering little stained hearts and praying to be cleansed again.

" Get up, children. We kneel only in prayer. Now tell me. Have you been happy? "

" No, oh no, no, no! "

" Do you think a few groundnuts were worth that unhappiness to us all? "

They stared dumbly at this new notion.

" Did we have a nice evening yesterday? "

" No, it was dreadful," " I cried myself to sleep," " We had no stories . . ." came many replies.

" Does doing wrong ever produce nice fruit? Thus we are deceived. You see it now? Then we will not let it make us miserable any longer. You are sorry, and so you are forgiven."

What a glorious, divine power to be able to lift from anyone, specially from the heart of a child, the intolerable sense of being chained to wrong done!

Hope and joy and freedom, used eagerly for service, reign once more in our Home.

* * * * *

Another little one has arrived, Saguna. She is Radha's salvage. Five or six years ago a shepherd woman in Bukkuru died, leaving this mite a few months old. Neither the old grandmother nor the father could deal with a "bottle-baby." I have met very few Indian women who can. Hand-fed babies always pine, this little thing was no exception; her wails disturbed their rest, what was to be done? We will sell her to the *Bogum* people, they concluded. The *Bogums* offered six rupees; it is their common practice to buy girl babies when they have the chance. The law forbids it, but who will take the trouble to inquire and to prosecute? Radha heard of it. Of law she knew nothing; but her heart went out to the child and the dreadful future. "Give her to me, I will look after her," she said to the father. But greed had fastened on his heart. "Will you give me the six rupees the *Bogum* people would give me?" he asked. Yes, she would. It was her whole month's allowance at that time. She paid it and received a melancholy little bundle.

When I heard of it I thought it one of the finest Christian deeds I had ever seen. Not the financial sacrifice, though it was heavy. But Radha was about sixty by then, rheumatism plagued her, a little ease would have been welcome, but Saguna had to be attended to day and night. She suffered from chronic catarrh of the stomach after all the bad and irregular feeding; how much care and labour this meant can be imagined. Radha's work in the houses could not be neglected, nor the baby left alone at home, it had to be carried on all her rounds. And how unattractive the little one was, save to the eyes of pity! May I never see such hopelessly miserable baby eyes again; a weak nerve-wearing wail was kept up all the time; the skin was wrinkled over fleshless little limbs, unhealthily the stomach protruded—so wretched was the whole aspect that I did not think she could live. " If she lives long enough to learn to smile you will have performed a miracle, Radha," I said, never thinking it could possibly happen.

But the noble old woman persevered. Saguna learned to smile, presently to walk, *and* to talk, and Radha came to some of her reward. For Saguna lustily imitated her doings. Radha's nightly meetings for Hindu women have been mentioned; Saguna discovered a kingdom of her own on the same lines.

A few weeks ago I was sitting in Radha's courtyard at sundown. The door in the wall, screening it from the street, opened; in marched Saguna and behind her ten or twelve children of the neighbourhood, most of them twice her size. I retired discreetly into a corner.

" Kneel down," commanded the youthful leader. Obediently the others knelt. She surveyed them critically. " Bend your heads. Shut your eyes. You "—this to a biggish boy—" bend your head properly. Now we will begin."

The prayer-meeting began. It consisted in Saguna leading them phrase by phrase, and the children repeating everything she said. Her only request from heaven was to bless every one she knows or has ever met. No one was forgotten. A former servant of mine, now dead, still reigned in her memory as " the kitchen *dhora*," and as such was prayed for. An English official visiting Bukkuru was included, though difficulties arose about defining the unknown. " What is the name of the English *dhora* who stood outside our school to-day ? " she inquired of Radha in the middle of her prayer. " How should I know ? " replied Radha comfortably. But Saguna was not to be baulked. " Bless the English *dhora* who stood outside our school to-day," she explained to the Lord. Every missionary she knows was remembered, all neighbours, and any of their relatives that she knew; the list was so great that she was not always equal to its long stretch. "Who else is there?" she paused doubtfully. "You have not said Marala Naraina yet, and his wife, and their baby," supplied the devoutly kneeling congregation; and these were duly presented for the favours of Providence. The overtaxed little memory betrayed her into vain repetitions sometimes; "You have said that one already," the audience remonstrated once, fearing perhaps an unfair share of blessing on the twice-mentioned, but maintaining perfect decorum. The cow came home in the middle; the little intercessors opened their eyes to see where she wanted to go and made room for her—the cow pushed through the meeting to her accustomed place, and the prayer proceeded. "Out of the mouths of babes hast Thou perfected praise," I said in my corner, deeply touched.

And now Saguna is here in the Home: "It is best for her" said Radha. "I am out so many hours a day," but the tears were in her eyes. That seemed to me the greatest sacrifice of all. Young life about them is the consolation of the old; the bereaved old, who know life so well and how it takes from us our treasures; the old, who cannot be comforted unless they are habituating themselves to unseen companionship.

"Now the children won't come," Radha mourned. "But it is best for her to go." So she disciplined her will to sacrifice afresh.

* * * * *

Jewel and Flower, who are always revolving round the bungalow on some excuse or other, I have named in my mind "Satellites." Flower is an extraordinarily reliable child. If one sets her a task, without fuss, or complacency, or any self-consciousness, she quickly completes it and does not mention it. "Who will dig round the oleanders?" I asked when several garden tasks were dist ibuted. Flower undertook it. I had forgotten about it myself, returning when it was almost dark a small person was discerned by the bushes alone; while joyous shouts came from the playground.

"Who is that?" I called.

"I," came Flower's voice.

"Why are you not playing with the others?"

"I had not finished here."

She has built a lovely little temple of complete trust in her in my heart; I think it must react on the whole Home.

Her sister redeems the family from too uncanny saintliness; it is Margaret. Margaret, sent to fetch or do something, will always find distractions by the way. A number of children were sent to collect cow-dung; all returned but Margaret. In the end she was discovered by a thorn thicket where her eyes, as quick as her ears, had perceived lovely white blossoms; there she sat on the ground with her lap full of them, deftly twisted into a long flower-chain, and who was I to scold her for beholding lilies when she ought to have beheld manure? But the other children who had worked hard would have felt it to be unfair; so Margaret lost the meed of praise dealt out to them and even came in for a little moral pointing that flower-chains are a happier thing *after* the fulfilment of duties. Self-denial is not her strong point at present. Flower always had her farthing ready for the Sunday collection; never Margaret. I felt sure the parents had given both equally; on inquiry Margaret confessed lightheartedly that all her share had gone in sweets.

On the flower-chain occasion Jewel and Flower returned with great loads. "We must go back and fetch more, for there is still a great deal. When we started we prayed, and we prayed as we went along—and look how much we found!" Bless their hearts. Who shall say that their little eyes were not the keener for that prayer and that expectation?

A few days ago I had no one to send with important registrations to the post. "Will you go?" I asked the Satellites. Andapur is fortunately a town sufficiently countrified to permit of girls being sent through its streets, and I believe that training in responsibility of many sorts, in conducting business and knowing their way about, should form part of their education. They are not, as so many Indian women are, even my Radha, to be helpless at stations about taking tickets, or ignorant of cart fares or coolie dues; the various business demands of daily life are to find them equipped. At the moment of being asked the children had just come back from school; the hour of play was at hand, but only alacrity could be discerned in their immediate response: "We should like to go!" On return they related that the postage was one anna more than I had given them; they possessed nothing. "What shall we do? We must go back and get it, but then it will miss the post the *ammagaru* wishes it to catch. What shall we do?" Did they pray again? They thought of the school conductress living near, got the anna from her and despatched the letter in time. Resourcefulness is developing!

Service seems the easiest to teach; in fact they seem always to have known it. It must be part of the children's kingdom which we poor grown-ups lose. During the hot weather the *punkah* coolie failed; two or three girls fought for the chance of filling his place; since then, every evening, shoals of verbal petitions assail me to be allowed to repeat the entrancing task.

The Satellites discovered how glad I was to get much-needed mending done. In their free hour at midday they came with smiling faces, "Is there any work for us to-day?"

"Yes, Flower, there is a tear in the silk dress. Will you darn it?"

Flower flew upstairs, bursting with pride and pleasure.

Jewel looked crestfallen. She knows Flower, who is several years older, can sew much better.

"Jewel, you know the dress I wore this morning?" Does she not know every stitch of apparel I possess! "I will show you where some hooks need sewing on." Her flying feet hardly touched the stairs, her whole little being was in a tremble of delight—what for? How horrible to be a grown-up, with a thousand concerns of my own; if other people asked me to sew their hooks on I am afraid I should do anything but tremble with delight. I don't want the Satellites ever to grow up and lose their kingdom and become like me!

It is more difficult to train them to imagine and to think than to serve. After prayers one evening I asked whether, during the past week, any girl had had anything to give her pleasure? Anything for which she would like to say "Thank you" to God? To God? Ah, that was difficult. What were the kind of things one thanked Him for? It must be along pious lines, of course. Though I put the question to each girl in turn no replies were elicited. "Rain," said one. "But that was the week before," others corrected her. "You had a headache and are better"—Jewel thought of this. That was all.

"Oh dear, what a Home!" I sighed. "Not a girl pleased with a thing! You seemed to get a lot of fun out of the cut grass you dragged into the Home—I see I made a mistake, you were really groaning. No doubt this House is a prison. I saw you squeeze your noses against the study window this morning and laugh when you saw the big doll sitting on the table, but that was pain, I expect. I saw you smelling the rose that opened to-day, that, too, made you miserable. And the stories you have now to read at midday—it is a wretched trouble to have to read them. What a house of unhappiness is this! I too, will now cry because there is no pleasure anywhere. I don't know what to think about your

Father in Heaven—here are twenty-five of His children and He has not given a pleasure to a single one for a whole week!"

"Oh, could we say those things?" "We didn't know!" "Ask us again!" "Next week we shall know a lot!"

Will they? It takes good eyes to perceive God's daily gifts.

* * * * *

Manikyam has come to the Home. Her mother died, her father deserted her; she ran wild in the village, begging, stealing, her hand against every man's. Relatives heard of this and brought her here. Now we all have our hands full. She fights freely, lies cheerfully; but a sturdy independence makes her attractive all the same.

For the Sunday class where each child says verses, she had learned nothing, not three words. I glanced round disapprovingly. "Has no one befriended her and taught her a text?"

"Indeed, we tried many times, she rolled on the floor and said, 'I can't learn, I cannot learn anything,'" came self-defending voices.

"Manikyam, come here." Cautiously she advanced, but came to a halt well out of my reach.

"Come nearer."

"I don't want to."

"Because you think I shall beat you? You need not be frightened."

But Manikyam has met little kindness or reason to trust people, and kept her distance. Whispers arose all round. "Go to her. She won't do anything. Really, she won't. Just go." Encouraged by friendly shoves she stood at last by my knee. We were having the lesson in the verandah.

"Look at the garden. Do you like it?"

"Yes."

"Who made it?"

"You." This baffling closure to intended revelation had to be swallowed.

"Do you see the big trees beyond? And the hill over there? And the sky? Who made them?"

"I don't know."

"Who do you think made you?"

"I don't know. I don't know anything."

"Well, I will tell you. . . ." (Here followed the sermon, if it may be called that.)

"*Now* do you think you could say 'The Lord is my Shepherd'?"

Next day came scandalized and puzzled defenders of the faith. "Last night Manikyam said, 'Tell me again who is God? *She* said there is God. I don't know who He is. Show Him to me.' When we said we could not she said, 'I don't believe He is anywhere.'"

Manikyam now haunts the study. She had little dirty habits at first which she abandoned in one great relinquishment and never repeated. But oh, her mischief! She picked the precious tomatoes ripening in the Home garden. Told to weed the badminton court she ran away to my garden and raped flowers. Spoken to after her crimes she looks at one with a disarming face of radiant joy, unrepentant, ready for any fray. I foresee that soon we shall all abandon every principle we ever possessed, and, revolving round Manikyam, turn into lawless pirates.

Yet I have great hopes of Manikyam.

For when I walk in the garden it is not flowers that move me the most deeply. It is the mystery and the miracle of seeds.

Surely happy is he and blessed above others who has the chance of sowing a seed in the heart of a child.

CHAPTER XXI

At dusk I was walking in the fields bordering the compound. A curious smoke-coloured haze hung in the west over a fiery oven brewing gold; suddenly from the furnace a great hand reached forth with fingers shooting flames, the eastern sky became stormy seas of rose and opal where shining streaks lead like celestial paths to the heavenly city in the heart of the sunset. As I stood gazing at " the glory that shall be revealed " plain to view here and now, two little girls came running towards me, children of the owners of a garden of date palms and vegetables a little farther on. " We have wanted to see you for such a long time! " they said shyly. One could imagine them watching the bungalow being built and weaving a mystery of romance about its strange inhabitant. They, in their turn, caused some thinking, —lonely children, living across the fields within two furlongs of the Home. After evening prayers in the Home I related the encounter and painted a few of the differences between my listeners and their little Hindu neighbours.

Three petitioners stood in my study next day. " Please may we go to the garden and teach those girls something ? " Later they returned with happy reports.

" First they had to comb their hair and look more tidy. Then we taught them about the birth of Jesus and one verse of a lyric. One girl learned very fast; but both said, ' More, more, tell us more stories! ' May we go several times a week ? May we bring them here and show them our Home ? "

Good little bridge builders! Finding fresh ways of contact between Christians and non-Christians is an aim always before us. Sometimes unexpected opportunities occur.

On Fridays one may see a fine mixture in the Home. From an adjoining compound come the daughters of the

Brahmin surgeon; the High School sends a contingent of girls with Rose, their fellow-pupil; from our own schools in the old town and the Extension arrive a medley of Brahmin and Sudra girls brought along by the Home children. The "drama" is the attraction; for a custom of acting Scripture stories has been instituted. It originated partly in the wish to add yet another element of joy to the children's lives; for what childhood can be stored too richly with happy memories? The main thought, however, was to stimulate imagination.

"You may not ask 'what story shall we act?' Or, 'how shall we dress up?' That is your business. You may look round on all the things I have and ask to borrow what you think you need."

The result sometimes astonished me. After a course of lessons in Acts, Peter in prison was chosen for one entertainment. A fine king draped in my red tablecloth gave orders; the courtyard door flew open and in marched six couples of amazing policemen; turbans, girdles, all splendid enough, but the truly impressive things were their swords,—the pods, fifteen to twenty inches long, of the flame-trees, what genius had thought of that? To see Martha, a big and rather stupid girl, conducting the meeting, enlivened by a perky little Rhoda, in Mary's house was also a pleasing surprise. In school she never by any chance had an answer, but the acting revealed that she had taken in something after all.

Another time the Old Testament was to the fore, Joseph in Egypt.

They could have given points to modern prison reform. Timid prisoners crouched between the wall and two backless benches. Joseph, which is also called Margaret, regarded them kindly. "I will tell you a story." One member of the audience felt nervous tremors, apprehending an anachronism, but Joseph had a clear sense of history. Abraham was his theme. The prisoners evinced scant interest and much scepticism.

" How could an old woman have a son ? "

" Well, she did. Put it in your mind."

Here the manager recognized her own phrase and tone of voice and sought to hide her shaking shoulders; fortunately no one paid the least attention to her, for the butler and baker were just arriving, causing a necessity to let out the walls of the prison a little. Joseph, unperturbed, continued his efforts to uplift the degraded classes. " I will tell you a story." But the butler and baker, as behoved royal courtiers, looked rather scornful, and presently let loose a torrent of higher criticism on the story of Isaac's sacrifice. " How could God order that ? Why did he go to be killed ? Where did he think the things were ? Did he expect a shop up the mountain ? " Poor Joseph, rather in a corner, took a firm stand on the plank of inspiration and said stoutly, " That is the story. What can *I* do ? It is written like that. Keep it in your minds. Now say after me . . ." Here followed a lyric in the learning of which the prisoners showed remarkable aptitude.

Pharaoh's feast followed; court grandees marched in after the queen (that the latter had just been Potiphar's wife and had no further queenly apparel disturbed no one) : Andapur baker's biscuits were handed round; dancers trooped in, also dunces who, by imitating naughty school children, gave Pharaoh royal entertainment, though royal dignity was hard put to it to maintain itself before an audience unrestrainedly convulsed; he had, however, enough self-control left to bestow *largesse* and to wave away the baker—or was it the butler ? Some girls newly come to our Home looked a little astonished at the freedom and laughter; for general games followed, Brahmin girls, Sudra girls, Christian girls, all tearing about and enjoying themselves together. Though not intended or even thought of it would seem that one result of our Home plays is a little nearer approach between Hindu and Christian girls, as well as between various strata of Indian society, who would not otherwise meet on a social basis.

The venture, however, has to be carefully watched in various ways. A small committee was put in charge of the dramas; their word was final in the distribution of parts. At the next acting I noticed the four on committee had the four chief rôles. Still, I don't despair of attaining to self-government.

The need of training in independent thinking was demonstrated at our last Church meeting when the women teachers copied my voting faithfully. Wherefore I abstained; then doubtful hands went up as far as uninspired noses, ready to go higher or come down again according to the lead given. The meeting was instructive in other ways; a delegate to the Telugu Church Council was to be chosen. The deacons submitted the name of Vedana (one of themselves), but the Church ultimately elected another man. Vedana, looking as black as thunder, seized his turban and walked out in a rage

From home we get interesting expressions of opinions as to the splendid results that will follow the granting of independence to the Indian Church, and no doubt these will come in time; but the bulk of our people need some training first!

Meditating thus I said last Sunday to the children, "To-day, instead of an ordinary lesson, shall we have a little talk?" They were very willing for this innovation.

"You played badminton yesterday?" asked an unsabbatic manager. "Who won?" Six or seven triumphant hands shot up.

"Who lost?" Six or seven dejected ones wriggled up slowly.

"Which is the chief thing, to win or to play?" came a catchy question.

"To win, win, win, to *win*!" they said, falling into the trap.

"Oh, to win. I see. The chief thing is to win. You who lost yesterday will not want to play to-morrow, of course!"

"Yes, yes, we want to play!"

"Why? You lost. You may lose again. The chief thing is to win. You did not win. If you cannot get the chief thing why should you want——"

Triumphant voices interrupted, "The chief thing is to play!"

"You have got that, have you? Now tell me, could you have played without the other side?"

"No, we could not."

"So although they beat you they gave you a good time?"

"Y-e-s."

"And they were pleased that they won?"

"They were!"

"Were you pleased to see them pleased?"

No answer at all this time, only hanging heads.

"Did any of you say to them, 'You gave us a good time, we had a fine game, you played well'?"

Astonished gazes met me. Then it was the turn of the victors who had listened with complacency.

To lose well, to win well, these are lessons which have yet to be learnt in this country. It is not uncommon at football or cricket matches for the umpire's decision to be questioned and the rival teams to fall quarrelling. Trivial as the above conversations may seem it is the kind of seed sowing that is needed all over India if a new spirit is to grow.

After our talk the children gazed as if becoming conscious of the dawn of a new ideal.

"You may all go now, only Jewel and Saguna stay behind."

An immediate and determined chorus arose. "We will

all stay behind!" (With regret one has to report that private interviews with the "Head" have no terrors for them.)

The Manager asked mildly, "Why do you want to stay?"

"You will teach them a new game," the suspicious children accused a delinquent of known habits.

"I have no such intention," they were assured.

"You will tell them a new story," they persisted unconvinced.

"No, I shall not tell them a story."

The children were nonplussed. They could think of nothing else that the missionary ever does. "Then what are you going to do?"

"I shall show them a work," said the missionary, yielding to pressure.

Wild and noisy triumph at having wormed a secret out of unwilling authority broke out in many voices. "We will all stay and do that work! We all, all, all, want to know what that work is, and we all want to do it!"

A lazy manager woke into sudden life. "You all want to do that work? That work has been with you for three months and no one did it. It said very softly, 'Please do me,' and you never heard. Anybody could have done it, but no one noticed that it had remained undone."

Absolute silence, not to say open-mouthed puzzledom, reigned.

"This is the work." I drew beside me a shy girl from another Mission. "Often when I come home I find you all playing and Lena looking on. I know you called two or three times 'Come and play,' but she still felt strange; so you let her get into a way of not joining you."

They went then—a little gravely; and the remaining two held a council of war—or peace?—on the best way of breaking down the walls of Lena's fearfulness.[1]

[1] Later on it was discovered the children had not been so remiss after all. Bad adenoids with the child in question were chiefly to blame.

The Scripture story-acting is going on its bridge-building way. The Prodigal Son was acted in the Mohammedan school before an audience of Hindu and Moslem women; the place was crowded. Incidentally the Christian girls are getting a little training in evangelistic work.

My little builders of the future, God grant that your own foundations be well and truly laid!

Unexpected opportunities for bridge building sometimes spring out of the mere brick and mortar. The school-house serves as a meeting-place in the evenings for a band of young men who intended first to form a Christian Endeavour Society; but it blossomed out into a Service League to which other religionists were brought. The first time these were invited the subject for the evening had been previously and, perhaps not very opportunely, fixed: how to present Christianity to Hindus. In the lecturer's view this work was to be done "in three ways; by being social, by leading pure lives, by an inspiring spirit." I tried very hard to gather what was understood by the last and perceived in the end it meant musical evangelistic meetings. A Mohammedan, an earnest-looking lad, got up and said, "We don't really know anything about Christianity." The others confessed to the same. The Christian young men, being invited to answer, became a little involved and wordy; the Mohammedan got up again, "Please, we want it plain."

It revealed how great is the opening in the student world of Andapur.

Sixteen young men, the majority non-Christians, signed their membership and now report various services done during the week.

Last time we heard that an evil-smelling well had been brought to the notice of the authorities; a lame bullock was taken out of the shafts and report threatened; several small boys were stopped from smoking; a man's feeble desire to keep away from the toddy shop on market day was successfully reinforced by a member of our Service League; a Hindu who had "a charming faculty" charmed away the pains of a scorpion sting.

Here are earnest and enthusiastic young men banded together for unselfish ends: wanted, a Leader.

While engrossed with the problem of finding time for young men the Inspectress of Schools arrived and brought afresh that of young women: "A young widow from Hindupet has joined the Government school here; can you look after her? She is but a child and her mother untrustworthy." When I went to see her the girl said frankly: "My mother is in a bad life, I cannot stay with her." An aunt has taken her in, not very willingly, as the family is poor. The neighbours drifted in to voice their opinion: "You must do something; how long can the relations feed her?" The pathetic sight was Subi herself, pluckily standing up to an adverse fate. "I never studied before; while my father lived he never would let me."

As he was an illiterate farmer he may be excused. But what about a young Brahmin matriculate who recently sent a peremptory message to his parents-in-law at Bukkuru: "I do not wish my wife to continue her studies," a little girl who had attained but to second standard? Here was Home Rule, Limited—with what prospects for the home?

* * * * *

From Subi who is at least of respectable farmer caste I went to the school and found Rukmini, of the dancing girls'; the poor child had to go through the ceremony in the temple when she was "married" to the god; but after that she made a stand and would not enter the career of the *Bogum*. She asked leave to go back to school and educate herself to be a teacher. The relations allowed it at first, but now they are tired of it. For over a month they have been pestering her every day to do as they do. She has to live with them; having no means of livelihood she is obliged to "eat their rice." It means living in a brothel, daily seeing and hearing things to vex her soul, and she only about sixteen or seventeen. As far as I know she has no wish to be a Christian; as for Subi, she knows nothing about our teaching yet, having come from another town, but both want to be good women. Have we not a duty towards them? Where Christian Missions are at work surely they should protect such as these; one of my dreams is a hostel for Hindu girls in the Mission compound.

Objections will be raised at once that Christian Missions cannot assume responsibility for all unprotected girls in a continent of millions, as they cannot finance a teacher in every unevangelized village.

No; but it is during the period of transition that demands are made on Western help. When the economically independent classes in India have been brought into the faith and obedience of Christ the monetary burden will no longer rest on the West. Perhaps in that day many from the West will regret nothing so much as their anxious economies, and none rejoice more thankfully than those countless unknown, though not unnoticed, helpers of whom it is recorded to-day as it was of a shy giver long ago: "She of her poverty has cast in all the living that she had." When I think of many a humble collector, many a struggling local missionary secretary, I think that, maybe, there will be another commendation like unto it: They, of their scant leisure, have given all the free time that they had, in helping towards realization the ideas dear to Christ's heart.

CHAPTER XXII

ON the platform at the little wayside station Erana brought tea. It tasted poor.

" Kettle not boiling, too windy," he explained.

" Why did you make the fire on the windy side? Does the wind come from four sides at once ? " I asked.

Sarcasm was wasted. He said gravely, " Yes, it comes from all four sides." I gave it up.

But now I think he was right after all.

A strange epidemic has broken out. " Bombay fever " they call it in the town, where half the population is ill. I hear that in many parts people are lying and dying by the roadside. The medical staff everywhere is depleted, doctors having been sent off to Mesopotamia. Hospitals in Bukkuru and Ramidi are closed. In these places influenza is raging. Several of our teachers there are ill. Now Raja Shekara, our Andapur pastor, is down. Next door to him Mitra, one of our Christians, and his wife and their three children are all helpless on their backs. Most of the children in the Boarding Home had gone home the previous week for the mid-term break of ten days; but six or seven whose homes are too distant were left. Fever is starting among them. Of those gone home Alice is back in hospital here; her family dragged themselves to Andapur, all of them ill and Alice delirious. Jaia, the headmistress, is down, so are her father and her sister. I am thankful when there is one member left in a family who can see to the rest. The trouble came upon us without warning. The children who went away well and strong are now in their villages going down with this terrible sickness. I have known nothing like it. Plague and cholera cannot compare with it, for these never mowed whole families down at once. Not that all die, but all are ill, no one is left to nurse or cook, and yet the most careful nursing is required. The whole Joshua family here are sick; in Gideon Simon's house all but Simon himself are ill, the mother and four children. The mother died.

I have to live not by the day, but by the moment. It means being out all day, going from one sick person to another. I entered Raja Shekara's house in cold fear; they had sent a message his heart was failing. As I came in I heard the women weeping and wailing and thought with a sinking heart he was gone. But we got him to rally, and hope lived again. They begged me to stay, for delirium started afresh, it was difficult to keep him on the bed; the members of the family are worn out with constant watching; in their deep anxiety they cannot be persuaded to take turns, and so all get exhausted.

Distances are a difficulty; it is nearly three miles from the pastor's house in the new town to the hospital in the old. There Alice's father died. The foolish mother went about loudly lamenting and wailing, leaving Alice alone. I came upon the child staggering about in delirium in the hospital compound. Another time I found her in the ward, needing water, moaning by herself, no one near. I longed to stay with the lonely girl; but there was Mitra and his family to be fed. A coolie is in their house; I live in fear lest he should bolt. It is a great thing to have him to attend to them, though he cannot be trusted with the preparation of the food. In between I rush back to the Home; as Dorcas the matron is with Raja Shekara there is no one in charge. Flower and Jewel are the ones left on their feet; they are bricks, beyond belief, doing everything, thinking of everything, keeping up bravely with next to no help or encouragement. Fortunately all five patients seem to have light attacks. Only once Jewel broke down: "We did all we could for them; you said they were not to have rice, so we made them gruel with no lumps or anything; they said it was too hot, we cooled it; then they said they would not eat it without sugar; we had no sugar. You were not there, no one was there; then I cried."

My heart was torn over them, but more torn over Raja Shekara; every available hour was spent there. The poor overheated brain caused all sorts of delusions; sometimes it took four or five of us to hold him on his mattress. I was there from three o'clock; once I went out for a breath of fresh air, that moment he was up and nearly out of the house. At 9.30 I had to go home for some food and rest; when just fallen asleep, a message of distress roused me, Raja Shekara could not swallow, they said, and I cycled there at midnight. Returning later on for a few hours' sleep I was awakened in the early morning by wails. Alice's mother had come to say the child died in the night.

I collected some flowers in the garden and cycled to the hospital in the old town; there was no one to make a coffin or procure cloth. We had only a mat to wrap the little body for its last resting-place, but the white blossoms redeemed all from sordidness. Everything had to be done under a sense of hurry and deep anxiety for Raja Shekara, and fretting to be with him quickly. When I reached his house in the new town I was met by the news that next door the wife of Mitra had died during the night, her little unborn child with her. The other three children seemed like to follow, lying there wan and helpless, their father at death's door too. The youngest girl rather clutched at my heartstrings in the docile way she always opened her mouth in response to my coaxing, and the lovely little thoughtfulness that made her lift a feeble hand to push her jacket out of the way when her sore chest was rubbed with ointment. A neighbouring Christian woman and I washed the corpse of the poor dead mother and prepared her for burial.

Then at last I could enter Raja Shekara's room; he was

rambling confusedly in several languages, but never failed to answer rapidly in English to my question, "Do you know me?" "Yes, I know you." So far, my name had always followed; but when I said this time, "Who am I?" his face took on a radiant look and he said loudly "Jesus!" My heart sank. Though quieter, he was already beyond our reach. He seemed to see or feel many presences, straining to look upwards he gasped, "Beautiful—beautiful—stars!" where the rest of us blind and earthbound mortals saw but a low and smoke-dimmed ceiling. "How many, many, brothers and sisters!" he called with a strong voice.

Still we struggled, still we hoped against hope. But in the end the brave heart stopped; I could feel no pulse, though the lungs fought for half an hour longer.

We are all dazed with grief.

* * * * *

I cannot write or think of him without burning tears. He was one who never failed any of us. I do not know that there is any other human being of whom I could say as of this beloved fellow-worker that never have I seen him in a mood that was not Christlike. Not once did I know him to seek his own, or betray by such subtle signs as a passing tone of voice, a quick look or expression, self-interest in any form. Amid countless incitements to it, slander, misunderstandings, quarrels in the Church, he exhibited no resentment. His humility was a wonder. I have known him to be unjustly blamed even by those who should have known him better. It is comparatively easy to be humble under praise, but under undeserved blame? Yet he achieved this rare distinction. That India, that the Christian Church in India, has produced such as he must inspire in us all "a virtue called fortitude,"[1] amid

[1] Paget, *Concerning Accidie*.

the ceaseless temptations to lose heart when one sees so many who "all seek their own."

* * * * *

The strain goes on. In the house the waterman and the gardener are ill, the one remaining pillar is cook, so that meals appear; but the garden is unwatered, and shrubs and flowers are left to die. From the town comes the ceaseless sound of tomtoms, indicating the removal of corpses. In the midst of so much illness and death I sometimes hardly realize which world I am in; anything seems possible, and the next life hardly a step away. I woke up in the verandah and saw the dawn creeping up; an old moon was standing over the hill and the tank [1] gleamed under a lightening sky; the farther hills were outlined sharply against the east. It was a scene of indescribable beauty; I caught myself asking in bewilderment which world is it? And slowly and regretfully realized it was still the old earth.

Heartrending news comes from villages where they are without medical aid of any sort; I was despatching some medicine to-day to an out-station and fell asleep in my chair doing it. Except for occasional exhaustion I feel perfectly well, though I should like to have the sight of drawn and sunk-in faces less impressed on my mind. Normal times with all their pressure seem a haven of rest now. Over Mitra death and I are still waging a daily fight, his fever remains high, but he has not collapsed. He is a fearfully fractious patient. His three little ones have turned the corner; the girls in the Home are better, but now Jewel is down. If anything happened to Jewel I think I should straightway give up the ghost myself. I read that this terrible influenza is stalking every village and town all over India; the papers say it is over the whole world.

At Koppala another child from our Home has died, dear

[1] Artificial lake.

little Ray; all her family are sick, the same bad news comes from all the villages, also pleas for help; but it is impossible to leave here just now. At every turn I long for Raja Shekara; I could not have believed I should have missed him so bitterly and with so aching a heart; only now does it appear how he mothered us all. He was so unobtrusive that we did not realize what a tower he was, nor how constantly we all turned to him. In each perplexity every one's instinct was "We must ask Raja Shekara." He was the soul of everything here.

His poor wife and the three little sons are now in this compound. The youngest is a lad of parts. Two ponies were feeding near the Home; out of it marched threateningly Soma Raj, aged about two and a half. Conscience doth make cowards even of ponies; they fled before the avenger who came on with his bare hands, though he used them to pick up and fling stones. The ponies' faster rate soon removed them out of range, but presently I noted them near the well, lapping up little pools of spilt water. Round the parapet of the well, unseen by them, crept Soma Raj, this time with a stick; suddenly he turned the corner and was right on them, brandishing his weapon like a forbidding archangel; the two sinners bolted at the gallop, the tiny creature after them, waving his flaming sword; never did ponies look such fools, or a wee boy so ridiculously superior; I felt grateful to him for making me laugh for the first time for many days.

Now, gradually, normal times are returning, and with them normal troubles. In the Church we are without a pastor, and how desperately Raja Shekara's beautiful and humble spirit is missed cannot be told. The government lies temporarily in the hands of the diaconate, men of little education and not much religious experience. One is a contractor, who is building our new school in the Extension and is, I fear, succumbing to the temptation to cheat. The Church secretary misconstrued his powers and made announcements that had not been discussed with the other deacons, who took offence at being set aside. When reminded of limitations he sent in a curt "Please get another secretary." Yet all desire the part of assisting in the Sunday services.

But when my heart was failing at so much shallowness and unreality it was cheered again by the presence of a new member in our congregation; an Indian professor transferred to the Government college in Andapur. The fine Christian spirit of this man, who belongs to a different denomination (awful word!), and is superior in education to our members here, yet joins enthusiastically not only in our services but in all other efforts for good, made my heart glow.

And even about the deacons let me not be tempted towards the injustice and wickedness of scorn. Who would be audacious enough to say what inner opportunities they really had, or what use they are making of them?

Yet I am aware that many spiritual perils are threatening our little community.

Some time ago a fellow-missionary was mourning to me over the quarrels among their Christians; I had said then, perhaps under the helping influence of Raja Shekara, I had not noticed it so much in Andapur. Retribution has overtaken me.

It began in the beloved Boarding Home where a difficult situation arose through Konamma, the barber girl. She had been persuaded to go to the Rescue Home in Mysore on the promise that if she did well there she should be allowed to come here afterwards. Here she has been for some months and, as feared, does not fit in. Her earnestness is quite real; she has many good desires and eagerly received instruction; her often repeated plea to be baptized was granted in the end, and she received a new name, Santoshạ, Joy. But the old nature is still in evidence; she has an ungovernable pride and temper which make it very difficult for the matron.

Both come with tales of intolerable woe, Santosha brought accusations of being scolded and abused, of being called a prostitute before the children. The matron spoke of a spirit of rebellion and disobedience, refusing to do tasks, meeting overtures with disrespect; of loud and wild talk, of children being ordered and even banged about. The difficulty of conducting the Home was unbearable; she would resign her post here and now. Santosha also came, ready to walk out of the house; no, she had nowhere to go, but she would get some work and be independent. An hour and a half I struggled with her, then had to leave for a deacons' meeting which in its turn made me feel as if little grinning devils were all round, scoffing and jeering " You cannot cast us out! " and indeed I could not. On return I sent for Jaiamma, the headmistress, to help me bring Santosha to a better mood. But Jaia in every way takes the part of Santosha, who is her convert and pet; every word of hers is believed; when the matron came in Jaia would not salaam to her and remained dumb as a post and as helpful—the interview was a failure. Unpeace between matron and Jaia threatens the whole work, for Jaia is headmistress in the day school to which the Home children go.

Already Jaia is wrought up over another friend of hers who worked in the Mission here and proved unsuitable; the finding of this proof is attributed to matron and the score against her is duly underlined. Depressed and perplexed I went to bed that night, seeing no way out.

For the present Santosha is kept in the bungalow; in the school she might conspire with Jaia, and perhaps corrupt girls on the way; in the Home another flare with matron might occur. Jaia wears the aspect of blackest thunder; a corresponding atmosphere pervades the school.

The fire spread. Jaia's father, a deacon, came in, bringing his resignation and a tale of grievances on his own account, going back through years and involving others; revealing an attitude of mind which appalled me. It seemed as if the veil were torn away for a moment, as if one could see the feelings our people harbour deep down; suspiciousness of one another, jealousy, hatred, deceit, even hypocrisy. And I, who go on believing in them, a simple fool. Ananda told me as much, disguised by the euphemism, "We all say Missiamma is without guile," though presently he was more explicit and charged me with not judging rightly.

"But don't you believe that matron tries to be good, that in spite of some failings she wants to follow Christ?" I asked desperately.

"No, I cannot say that."

"That lack of faith is the worst injury you can do her!" I cried out.

But he did not know what I was talking about.

It is, as Clutton Brock implies in one of his books, that they judge one another's values by their conduct—though they don't so judge their own. They see the outburst of temper and condemn *in toto*; and truly, the things these people say when in a temper are rather terrible. All their heathen ancestry, all the present atmosphere of the bazaar comes surging up. However, one may learn from Shakespeare that they used similar language in Christian England a few centuries ago. A few centuries hence things may be different in Christian India!

Ratnappa followed. Was I going to put Nilamma back in her work?

"How can I, while she sticks to proved falsehood?" I replied.

"But why rake that up again?" he asked. "Should you not forgive?"

"The lie, adhered to, would fester in her," I explained.

"If she confesses will you put her back?" he urged.

The utter blindness shocked me. Confession from a purely utilitarian motive would, in his eyes, render her quite fit again to teach Christian truths. He would go to her and say, " Confess, and you will get the work back."

When cycling to school after this interview I sent up a prayer of gratitude to Peter for his lying and swearing, and going on lying and swearing even after years of Christ's companionship. Equally thankfully I addressed the other disciples, for quarrelling by the way and being sensitive about their dignity, for every bad, mean, cowardly thing they ever did, and every stupidity they evinced about Christ's aims. These were all so many rays of comfort: I even yearned for more, and turned in my mind to the Corinthians who satisfied my thirst for badness. Truly, I don't want to hear about saints at all; or if I do, let it be about their sins and limitations, it is these which fill me with hope.

Meanwhile, how on earth am I to get along with so many resignations and vacancies ?

* * * * *

The still more immediate problem has become how to get along at all. Lumbago has gripped me, things on the floor are as much out of my reach as heaven, and I am chained to the couch. . . .

Santosha has marched in, bringing my gold pencil, found by her in her box (unlocked). Someone had put it there, to throw suspicion on her, she declared. Who could ? The children ? There might be a little thief, but they would surely put it into their own box. Teachers and matron never come into the room unless I am there. I think Santosha enacted this little drama to prove how much ill-will there is against her; she herself had every chance of taking it while she sat here sewing.

She was followed by Nilamma, asking to be taken back into the work. " Are there no words to be said before you say that ? " I asked.

" No. What other words are to be said I have said to

God. It is not for anyone to judge me, it is between me and God."

She has not a conception of what we should call ordinary morality. She, like Santosha, is a convert from Hinduism.

There is an idea abroad that converts, simply because they are converts and have left an old faith for a new, must be better representatives of Christianity than those to whom its truths have long been familiar. They are credited with the virtues of saints, the fortitude of martyrs, the untiring enthusiasm of idealists. Whereas, generally speaking, while faithfully following a new gleam of light and proving their loyalty to Jesus Christ often by heroic sacrifices, they also bring with them the deeply-rooted habits and ideas of their former atmosphere. The grandeur of the Christian character is not attained by any of us at a leap; certainly not by those handicapped by the delusions, disorders, and darknesses of their old environment. More than ever one is impressed by the importance of Christian institutions, and of instilling Christian standards into minds still plastic.

A difficult peace has been patched up; I feel it to be, rather, an armed truce.[1]

But when the atmosphere appeared very heavy, little rays of light broke through. A timid cough sounded from the verandah. "Who is it?" I called. Uncertain shuffling followed. "Come in!" A shy, pretty girl entered, Honura, sister of a Ramidi schoolboy. She has come here to help the Ramidi headmistress who has to undergo treatment for her eyes. She was all eagerness and shyness and pleasure and diffidence, coming by degrees out of her shell.

"I was frightened to come and see you. But how much I like being here! It is like nothing I have ever seen. Our people—they never talk to one another like they do here, they are rude and rough, you could never think how rude.

[1] Later on Santosha was sent to be trained as a nurse. She is working now, fully qualified, in a Mission hospital.

But here, how kindly they all talk to me! I never saw people so polite and kind. I want to stay here and be a Christian."

What looked murky black to me appeared snowy white to her.

The poor girl is only sixteen, and a deserted wife. I learned she had a younger sister, about thirteen—an expectant mother! "Yes, she is quite a child, the little one. But our people are like that," Honura added simply. Her own future causes me concern.

Another visitor arrived, a student in the Teachers' Training School here. He brought news of a Hindu girl, a fellow-student in the same school whom he influenced, and who now wants to become a Christian. There was a fracas in the school about it. The headmaster upbraided him, all sorts of petty persecutions followed. But the enthusiasm of this youth is unquenchable.

"I want all India to become Christian. They *must*! Moreover, I will bring them. At least I will bring a great many. I don't want Mission pay, I shall get Government work and then evangelize in my spare time. I will bring them! In the training school I tried to win one man, he went back; another, he went back too, but now Rangamma is firm. There will always be some remaining among those I bring."

His eager confidence was most refreshing.

There was yet more to hear about Rangamma. The girl's parents are well-to-do, they have fruit and vegetable gardens which bring in a comfortable competence. Nevertheless they are bent on getting this widowed daughter off their hands. Illiterate themselves, they do not understand that a teacher's profession means a livelihood; they went to the headmaster of the Training School and asked him to "find a rich young man who will keep our daughter." The callousness and blindness to any moral standard revealed by this open and barefaced demand seemed almost incredible. The headmaster, a non-Brahmin who takes his calling seriously, to their astonishment, severely upbraided the parents.

"Since then he has quite turned round about the girl becoming a Christian," said David. "Instead of abusing me he praises me for having done well to influence her. Now he is to be transferred. He called Rangamma privately and warned her: 'Mind you go to the Christians. Join them, otherwise there is no hope for you.'"

Sanctuary! Even in the eyes of a man who had violently opposed us at first.

But it will be seen that if Rangamma were to come, from such parents, from such an atmosphere, having caught a little light and a little enthusiasm from David, everything would yet remain to be done in the formation, even the conception, of Christian character.

"Until the whole is leavened." The daring confidence of that "until"! Out here, often, the dough seems more like stone and the leaven intolerably slow.

Then I think of Raja Shekara the beloved, and his almost perfect representation of Christ in our midst. Dwelling on the thought of him a great hope arises, and looking at these others I dare to repeat after Him, "Until"

CHAPTER XXIII

FROM the verandah came the familiar sound of a cough craving attention; the *peon* held out a notice, " Please sign; notice of a meeting to-night."

Whether we are politicians or not, time moves us on. Education is now " a transferred subject "; i.e. largely under Indian control. All schools are henceforward under the District Educational Council, on which Missions also are represented. Through a stifling evening I marched off to attend my first meeting of the D.E.C.

Mr. Srini Vasa Iyer, vigorously chewing betel-nut, occupied the Chair. As vice-president he was holding the fort till the president felt inclined to put in an appearance. He had all the agenda ready, so ready that the meeting was practically a farce. To be sure, at one point two members, each a president of a Taluk Board, but violently opposed to each other, insisted on airing their views; neither, though gifted with tongues, was burdened by any obligation to speak to the Chair, only by the necessity of bursting in upon his opponent's talk when he paused for breath. The rest of the meeting got tired of the duet, or duel, and talked to each other; the Chair lounged and chewed betel and made occasional entries. To him the matter was a foregone conclusion, but he let them talk until he thought they had had sufficient innings, when he interrupted the flow by saying " Then shall we put it down so ? " (I noticed that he had already put it down.) The meeting, to prevent the duellists from talking again, hurriedly said " Yes," or said something, or nothing; anyhow those two had to subside. Then the real president came in, our Collector, a Mohammedan. Two members rose politely as he entered; the rest went on sitting and talking; but the Collector did not seem to mind. He also liked betel-nut it appeared. Srini Vasa Iyer whispered instructions to him, the rest of the resolutions were read through, passed by the meeting in silence, or in private conversations. In another few minutes we were out.

Like everything else, the conduct of public meetings has to be learned. Even in backward Andapur this Rome will be built in time, no doubt. Meanwhile I perceive that the agenda has to be studied very carefully beforehand, for the meeting itself gives one little chance; at present the president, or rather Srini Vasa Iyer, does precisely what he likes.

What the Council liked, the agenda of another meeting showed. It contained a proposal that all Board schools should henceforth keep Sunday as a regular school day and have, instead, fortnightly holidays on new-moon and full-moon days. I learned that this practice was already introduced in some *taluks* of our district and was now to be ratified by regular legislation. Letters had come from Christian teachers serving in Board schools, complaining of the hardship entailed by this new practice.

Under British control the high days and holy days of Hindus and Mohammedans are always school holidays. Is Sunday opening going to be a sample of the treatment of minorities under Indian rule?

When the matter came up in the Council there was no lounging. Notice of a counter proposal had been sent in. But it was a fight with my back to the wall. I became conscious of intangible forces closing in from all sides. Race feeling, sex feeling, religious feeling, these three strongest human instincts were aroused. Reason—the defence of one day's rest in seven as a proved necessity; fairness to other people's consciences, neither of these could take the field against such opponents; the matter was a foregone conclusion. In Eastern fashion, however, my proposal was not refused directly, but referred to the Taluk Board There, of course, it has not the ghost of a chance. For the present then, Board schools still continue to be held on Sundays.

But no battle is lost while the defeated go on fighting. Protest has been sent in to the central provincial authority, still reigning above District Educational Councils.

* * * * *

Months have passed; the Missionary Educational Council of Madras took action against the performances in our district and similar deeds in a neighbouring one. These things take time in India. But Sunday being still a statutory holiday the matter was ultimately rectified, and our District Educational Council rescinded its resolution.

* * * * *

But by no means do we always meet educated Hindus as opponents. There are satisfying times when we can meet them, happily, as ordinary friends.

For long had Mr. Rangavachari been pressed to accept hospitality from a missionary; at last his engagements and mine could be made to square; I am enjoying the great pleasure of having him as a guest in my house for a few days. In the evening he read to me from Tagore's *Gitanjali.* " He comes, comes, ever comes." His comments on the poem were illuminating. " When I arrived you heard my cart coming through the lane. A creaking, ugly noise. One often hears it; it means nothing. But last night it signified to you the coming of a friend; it was neither ugly nor meaningless, because you were waiting for me. So with all things common or ordinary, ' He comes, comes, ever comes.' If you expect Him."

Here is ground where we can meet. But in other ways shall we ever learn to understand one another ?

" You English are so different from us," said Mrs. Ranga Sami Iyer. " The Judge's lady has children at home.

We could not be separated like that. When my son is a little late from school I grow uneasy; *peons* are sent to search for him; we must always see our children. But you English are different, you can let them go and be quite happy."

Half the world here certainly does not know how the other half lives—or suffers.

And even the possible approaches between East and West are often left unused.

In the train I met a delightful Englishwoman who told me she could speak Telugu. This was further explained to mean she could say "Where is the *toddy* shop?" Her husband is the official who inspects these places; the pair travel all over the district, he riding, she driving; on arrival at a village she trots out this phrase to find out whether her husband is there. I pictured the effect it would have on the villagers—an Englishwoman in the wilds of India, hurling at a gaping crowd this question which, doubtless, to them expressed the one desire of her heart! Her bravery impressed me, in thus travelling about; at the same time I felt green with envy at her leisure and chances to be in the villages. What endless opportunities, perhaps not even perceived—for bridging gulfs! Is there not some waste here of the fine material of English womanhood in India? If the British *Raj* had realized in time what avenues to the hearts of the people were open through women—if (I am, perhaps, presuming greatly) women's wit had been allowed a chance to exercise itself upon this problem, might not some way of using much latent force have been discovered?

Or is the missionary solution the only one?

* * * * *

Another honoured Indian guest has arrived; met first in England and now a professor of science in the new Mohammedan University of Alighar. Science brought him face to face with negation in religious matters, and in consequence a great melancholy pervades a sensitive and loving personality. As we sat in the verandah in the moonlight many thoughts found utterance; the most impressive was again one on cleavage, but not between East and West.

"I do not know what will be the future of the religion to which I nominally, though in no sense truly, belong. It is a curious irony that the university which was founded with the intention of propping up Islam is doing much to undermine it. Professors teach their subjects, but nothing else; the teaching of religion is entrusted to *Moulvies*, often ignorant and uneducated men who cannot keep order in their classes, and at whom the students laugh openly. Thus no religious ideals are presented to them."

"But you, yourself, could you not impress on them the imperiousness of the demands of the spirit?" I urged anxiously.

"I have nothing to teach them along these lines; I have no light myself," he replied sadly.

What a chance, in that North Indian University, for someone who has!

CHAPTER XXIV

ONE morning, during a stay on the hills, I was returning from a walk along a sunny and dusty road. Passing by a compound I noticed what seemed to be smoke from a fire. But the smoke condensed into a compact ball which tore itself from its surroundings and sailed towards me; it was a gay little cloud that, to my fatigue, seemed like a gentle greeting of heaven; white and dainty it came straight on and wrapped me round with its cool moisture, giving me time to kiss it and be blessed by it before I was through. Its sisters were hanging round the tops of the blue gum-trees, rather more elderly spinsters these, somewhat ragged and thin; my little friend floated up to them and was lost in their embrace, having fulfilled its mission. The next curve of the road hid all; yet the memory of an unexpected boon remained.

* * * * *

The years are passing, the road is tiring. Of little things and duties there seem to be very many; of the great things one hoped to do none at all. The modern spirit has caught us; it is a simple fact that all of us have too much to do. The schools, the Biblewomen, the Boarding Home are each scope enough for one person's energies, especially as the two first items are in half a dozen centres, involving tedious journeys; the Church, again without a pastor, claims time and much else; then there are nearly always new buildings to be put up, besides old ones to be kept in repair; the work among high caste women must not be neglected; visitors of all grades must be welcomed; a niche has to be found for correspondence and accounts; the household claims attention, not to speak of the garden; there is a certain amount of public work on educational and municipal councils, and withal the things no man can number, the interruptions. For all these there is one poor creature [1] who, in Macdonald's phrase, has to say often enough: "Remember, Lord, Thou hast not made me good." And all the time her real dream of mission work is to sit among the people and talk about the Rule of God in men's hearts. Dorcas often said reproachfully, "The women are asking for you," and I have to reply despondingly, "Next week."

"Every good gift and every perfect gift . . ." why not time, then, for such visits? Somehow, time came. Dorcas took me to a *Reddi's* house; in a cool, large hall, stone flagged, women sat in silken *saris* and many jewels; seeing their splendour I thought for a moment it might be a time to tread cautiously; though why one should think the rich invariably rather inaccessible I do not know; these rich certainly were profoundly eager listeners. They had bought a New Testament and read with great interest and intelligence the Sermon on the Mount. The last part, the unassailability of a life whose every action is based on the will of God, occupied our attention; almost one could perceive the glow of their responsive hearts. "I shall never forget this," said one young woman. "To-morrow I am going back to my husband's house; we live in a village where no one ever comes to teach us; I take this book with me, and your words in my heart."

Ramakka's house was the next, an old pupil who wants to come back to school because her husband is quite indifferent to her. Since her baby was born eight or nine months ago, he has made no move to call her back from her parents' house; he sent her neither money nor the customary cloth, nor even asked after his little son. She sat there with her baby, looking desolate. "I have not any refuge anywhere,"

[1] The married missionary had been transferred to another district, the claims of which were even more urgent.

she said dismally. " I want to come back to school now and train for a teacher; can my parents go on keeping me? But *he* is against it."

Frank revolt was the remedy I urged. " Come to school; if he hears and sends a message to forbid it say, ' I will fulfil my duty as a wife and obey, if you fulfil your duty as a husband and call me to your house.' " To issue commands but take no responsibility is an unfairness to which it seemed wrong to submit; but the women are so used to accepting it that it is almost impossible to rouse their spirits. Some day the retribution which always overtakes tyrannies will overtake this one.

In these days one may see it overtake an ancient tyranny, that of Brahmins. Since the British *Raj* began, this caste has managed to secure for its own members practically every appointment in the various Government departments. An outcry has arisen over this now; the non-Brahmin castes are demanding their share. The justice of their claim is recognized by authority. Only yesterday a Brahmin student from Ramidi, who had failed in his Matric., stood in my study, asking advice about his future.

" You could go in for Secondary Teachers' training," I suggested as a career. " I know they have taken some failed Matrics here in the College."

" Not Brahmins," he replied. " They take others and are not particular, as Government insists on non-Brahmins being trained now and makes allowances for them. But Brahmins have to fulfil every possible condition." Vengeance has begun; so long Brahmins excluded others, now they have begun to be excluded. And the injustice to Indian women will react one day on those who oppressed them; may that future generation of Indian men and women have learnt the mind of Christ before then and avoid many mistakes and much tragedy.

A widowed girl of about nineteen met us in the next

house; the parents would not allow her to return to school. "It is not the custom among our *Moodliar* caste to let young women go out alone." So here she must mourn a useless life away in the stuffy little courtyard. She looked at me appealingly. "Please do something," she whispered; "I want to come." As if by one magic stroke one could demolish impenetrable, unclimbable walls of thick ignorance and misapprehension, or sheer tyranny. The whole atmosphere must be attacked and it needs many of us.

In a Mohammedan house sat Hussein Bi, a young widow who lives with two brothers; they are always casting it up to her that she does not earn enough to feed herself; I allowed her a small scholarship to enable her to go on studying in the hope of a teacher's livelihood later on. Now another Mohammedan woman caught hold of me: "There is my daughter, Rasula Bi, her husband died suddenly; what will be her fate? Please do something."

"Please do something," echoed Rasula herself.

"Please do something," I also want to echo. To whom? A Committee?

But sometimes things move without a Committee.

A Brahmin house had specially requested a visit; next door lived another old schoolgirl of the weaver caste. It was market day. A number of relations, men and women who had come in from villages near, were sitting about. It seemed an opportunity not to be missed. Dorcas started on the man at Bethesda, and I followed it up. "To you also—'nearer is He than breathing, closer than hands or feet.'" The people sat spellbound; it surely is true what I lately read: "God within all these people . . . striving to make Himself known"; for it seemed as if they recognized Him when they heard of Him. "Never will I forget it, never," said one villager. Is not Augustine's great phrase true? "God is a sigh in the depth of every soul."

"What about the Brahmins' house?" I inquired.

"Yes, come, come." To my surprise, the weaver girl knocked at the door of the Brahmins' household and entered with us. We learned that she, enthusiastic about the Christian teaching learned at school, had done a little evangelistic work of her own, not daunted by the neighbours' superior caste. Two young women in glowing green and orange *saris* rose to greet us. Their appearance suggested worldliness; yet they too were reading the New Testament, and listened with the profoundest interest. It was not all the weaver girl's doing. "Our mother has been teaching us these things."

"Your mother?" I gasped.

"Yes. Her birthplace is on the east coast where she learned to read in a Mission school. She often says 'I will never worship any god, only Jesus Christ. All through my married life I have served only Him!' How sorry she will be to have missed your visit."

I looked again round the little room, and in my heart took off my shoes. Here was lonely courageous following, lonely patient prayer, lonely faithful teaching of her children. Well says Tagore:

> "I lay upon my idle bed,
> And I thought all work had ceased.
> In the morning behold, the garden was
> full of wonders of flowers."

How little, how very little time there had been for visiting of recent years! Yet here was a glimpse of a "garden full of wonders of flowers."

But, somewhere on the east coast, someone had to have time to keep a little Mission school. It is schools that have made all the opportunities I found in this afternoon's visiting.

Then let us take up the burden of them with fresh courage!

There was need; for into that very hour of joy crashed the news of teachers' quarrels. Straight from the Brahmins' house I had to go to the Mohammedan school and found unpeace and complaint. One woman was almost in hysterics at what another had said. The Divine spark in them is well overlaid, poor things!

The day began to decline; I battled my way home through the wind and dust; dark had fallen when I arrived and was met by the message: "The Salt officer's *peons* have taken the cow and bull off to the pound." The cowman had fever and stayed away; the cook was indulging his love of gossip in the bazaar; the last remaining prop of the establishment went off after the quadrupeds strayed from the paths of virtue. I sank into a deck-chair in the garden, hoping for a quiet half-hour.

A shadow fell over the pathway of lantern light from the verandah, a voice called. It was Mr. Rangavachari, always sure of a warm welcome. There were some questions to ask him to-day.

"Three girls in Dharmpalli whose parents have died suddenly from influenza are alone in the house and live by begging; will you take them into your Widows' and Children's Home? Our Committee will not allow me to take them here; ours is not an orphanage, but a home for the daughters of Christian villagers."

"What caste?" he asked.

"*Madigas*." [1]

"I am very sorry, we do not take *Madigas*."

So, somewhere, we reach limits in the best and most liberal-minded of Hindu efforts, I thought. "I will give you two or three addresses where they do," my unspoken thought was answered. If any caste Hindus have an orphanage where *Madigas* are received the great mountain of Hinduism is certainly moving perceptibly on its way to the sea!

He stayed till nine, giving the cook a chance to hear the very latest news in bazaar and produce a dinner also; the cattle too were called home across the sands of Andapur at a sacrifice of eight annas instead of golden hair. I went

[1] Low caste.

upstairs, tired, and then India gave more of her surprise. While I stood brushing my hair by a looking-glass facing an Eastern window, thinking of nothing in particular, I glanced into the mirror and there saw, reflected, a landscape of unearthly beauty; the Andapur hill stood sharply outlined against the night sky which grew lighter every moment; slowly the moon rose above the great rock till its golden globe hung in the middle of my looking-glass, while I stood, brush in hand, lost in wonder.

> "For a moment on the soul
> Falls the rest that maketh whole,
> Falls the endless peace." [1]

* * * * *

In the educated homes of Andapur the women are moving with the times. A *Samaj* [2] or two have been started whose members meet weekly. The *Sarada Samaj* is a very strict Hindu one; it was with some trepidation that I accepted an invitation to visit it. I expected something of a solemn religious nature. But there was little to distinguish it from an ordinary social gathering with a literary flavour. One lady read—or rather, intoned—in the usual sing-song style which makes it difficult to catch the meaning, a story from the *Ramayana* about a hunter in the forest. Nobody was listening. Conversations with children were carried on, also with one another; I caught artless remarks about myself. Goings out and comings in continued all the time, perturbing no one but a foolish Western visitor with a mind for order and notions about polite attentions to the reading of the hostess.

Toward the end the customary *kankanam*, the sacred red powder, was passed round; every one dabbed it carefully on the forehead as a mark of having performed a religious ceremony; but what religion had there been in it? The

[1] Myers, *Sunrise*. [2] Society.

chanting lady liked chanting; the rest liked meeting one another; the added sense of religious merit no doubt enhanced the pleasure; but for any realization of the Divine one looked in vain.

Indeed, the immediate and visible occupied them much more; when *tambulam*[1] was distributed one member began to hold forth on the many merits and the great name I had—earned, it appeared, by the giving of dolls at school prize-givings. Attentively I listened for praise of a more sustaining nature; but, instead, heard the name of a neighbouring station and was forced to conclude the speaker was confusing me with Mrs. Stephens of Guttur, so that even the rag of righteousness conferred by dolls was wrested from my clinging hands.

I was disappointed in the meeting; it seemed to emphasize the cleavage Hinduism so often presents between religion and ordinary life; the mere fact of a mythological story being read rendered it, in their eyes, a religious one; but what could they glean from it to feed those secret springs which must sustain them in their daily lives ?

The other Women's *Samaj* is a theosophical one in name, but seeing that its members are all Hindus it also has a strong religious bias in favour of Hinduism. They are however, very liberal-minded. Adiamma, the moving spirit among them, after studying the Gospel of Luke gave a lecture on the life and death of Jesus Christ. Also invitations to "lecture" at their gathering whenever she could were sent to the missionary. As often as time can be found for it this is now being done. A very different atmosphere meets one here from that in the *Sarada Samaj*; one of eager receptivity and even spiritual earnestness. "It is our festival," they said on one occasion when I found the room crowded, "but we have left the cooking and all other things to hear the words." There were widows and married women

[1] Betel-leaf and nut and a little lime.

and young girls sitting round, all but the first in glowingly coloured silk *saris*, orange, green, crimson; golden chains and jewels flashed everywhere; a little lamp burned before a gaudy print representing Saraswati, while a plainly attired missionary sat in their midst with the New Testament in her hand from which illustrations to which all listened respectfully were read at intervals.[1]

"You tell it us plainly and clearly; the bits are broken up for us, we need only put them into our mouths," they said. Another time three or four Hindu ladies were sitting in my garden.

"That good part," one of them remarked suddenly, "'that good part'; I cannot forget those words. When I sit down to my cooking, when I am alone, when with others, it ceaselessly rings in my mind: 'One thing is needful. Mary has chosen that good part'; I want, oh I also want that good part!"

"The same subject [2] you talked of I have spoken about in every meeting since," Adiamma reported. It made one realize how they hunger for the same mental and spiritual stimulus and food for which I turn to many authors (in such moments as may be snatched from the daily whirl, like meal-times, train journeys, and the like). The Christian literature of centuries is ready to my hand to help me on; but what is ready to theirs?

As I sat in their midst, or heard the pressing invitation afterwards to come again soon, memories came to me of former years; of efforts to get the women of Andapur to establish some meeting among themselves to which one might present a distinctly Christian message; how hard the struggle was; how unsuccessful; how beginnings were made and always came to an end again; how often the pressure of other work caused efforts to be relaxed, and even dreams

[1] *Our Daily Life and Religion,* Christian Literature Society, Madras, contains the kind of talks we had together.

[2] It was Chap. I in *ibid.*

to be abandoned or, at all events, to be pushed into the background—yet here it had come to pass, all of itself it seemed. Was it not another illustration of Tagore's lines? When I "thought all effort had ceased . . . behold, the garden was full of wonders of flowers."

* * * * *

Two Brahmin visitors have just left, members of this theosophical *Samaj*. They came to tell me that the *Sarada Samaj* had had itself registered as a Society and had received a Government grant for books and were expecting a further one for a building. The worldly success of the rival *Samaj* evidently rankled a little. Should we not get ours registered also?

"But do we want a grant?" I asked. "We come together to learn *bhakti*, true religion. How would money help us?"

"Would it not help to establish our *Samaj* more firmly? The *Sircars* would be behind it."

"And if they were?" I asked. "What we need are leaders capable of imparting to us religious truth. If there are such your *Samaj* will go on; if there are not what can all the Government support in the world do for us?"

Still Adiamma was inclined to yearn for it.

"See here, Adiamma. Is not what we want spiritual fruit? Now let us be sure, absolutely sure, of this: that *never* can there be spiritual fruits from other than spiritual roots."

Hardly had I said this when the other visitor, a widow who had sat by in silence, seized my hand with both her own while tears rained down her cheeks.

"That is it! It is the very truth!" she stammered, evidently under the stress of deep emotion, her soul shining through her tears.

Like the little cloud that distant day on the Palni hills, cool and refreshing on a dusty road, the Brahmin woman's instantaneous recognition of a spiritual law wrapped me round like a greeting of heaven.

CHAPTER XXV

Colleagues have arrived at last, an Indian woman and an English one, and with them the fresh realization that my farewell to India and her dear people is drawing very near. Speaking of the Home yesterday our new Indian helper expressed surprise and pleasure at the joyousness of the girls and their eagerness to perform any service that comes their way. "Is it because they are trusted?" she asked. "You seem to expect them to be good." Naturally I do. How can a child flourish in any atmosphere but that of trust?

What more can be done for these precious children? As I see my days with them slipping into the past I ask this anxiously over and over again. During the last holidays on the hills I tried to write for them some of the thoughts that I myself live by, to speak to them of great things in very simple words. These are now in the press. There are many other schemes and plans crowding into my brain, but for them the day is too far spent, and I can only hope now that the seed sown in their young lives has been truly good seed.

There is one habit we have tried to teach them that I confidently hope may be a fruitful one. For some years now a daily practice of ten minutes' silence has been observed in the Home before evening prayers; the girls may sit, or kneel, be inside, or outside, as they prefer; the one requisite is silence. The suggestion is to use the silence for thinking about God and the life He wishes us to lead.

Non-Christian India tends to live in the crowd. Spiritual recollectedness—hard to attain without solitude and silence, yet imperative for soul growth—is considered the part of the ascetic. In Christian Missions, where perhaps we do not lack object lessons in altruistic endeavour, we yet seem to miss those that emphasize the supreme need of inner spiritual activity. In this regard India has a great heritage; but the divorce she creates between common life and high religious attainment is a fatal one. The marvel of the union of Eastern and Western ideals in Christ forces one afresh to worship Him. May our daily ten minutes of purposed silence help to start in these little ones "the practice of the presence of God."

* * * * *

Several things in the Home lately have brought fresh encouragement. Some of the girls had been visiting a sick Christian teacher in the hospital and there noticed a village woman suffering from hip disease; of their own accord they saved up their scanty pocket-money to bring the lonely patient a gift of flowers and sweets.

Jewel came back from a holiday with relatives living some miles beyond our last outpost of Christian teachers, and described how one day she had started telling the neighbours' children some gospel stories. The neighbours themselves began to listen, and every evening afterwards they had eagerly asked for more stories and for prayer and singing of Christian hymns. So night by night she had given them what she could. Bless the little evangelist, though her simple recital tore the heart afresh. The many uncared-for villages and their waiting harvest!

In our Sunday classes, where a practice of five minutes' composition in answer to a "think question" has been started, the question, "What is the Kingdom of God?" revealed a general impression among the girls that it meant heaven. But Margaret, the clear thinker, wrote, "The Kingdom of God is where God rules," a definition that in its simplicity and comprehensiveness would surely be difficult to better.

Such signs, small as they are, of unselfish practical helpfulness, of (perhaps hardly conscious) evangelistic zeal, of right thinking, are as great a joy as the recent receiving into the Church of a little group of older girls. A very simple creed and confession had been placed in the hand of each. After a course of instructions they were asked to think it over and let me know if they were prepared to make these promises. They came after a week and said, "We want further time, please, to think a little more." This desire for reflection looked as if they understood something of the need for reality in personal religion, and I thanked God.

* * * * *

I have returned from a church packed with women; we are in the midst of great gatherings in our chief Telugu station, celebrating the centenary of our Society's work in the Telugu country. It is good to meet so many fellow-workers; good to see the crowd of Indian women in the church; perhaps the most impressive sight of all was the sea of faces in the large *pandall* erected for these wonderful meetings. I gazed and gazed on that great multitude, listening to speakers from east and west who had come from many missions and churches and denominations, to honour with us the work God has done in our midst. As I looked from the vast crowd seated before us back to the platform of missionaries old and young, a sense stole over me of unseen presences; here in this place had beloved Wardlaw Thompson met the South Indian missionaries of his day; here had others laboured and suffered and spent themselves; H. W. Campbell and those before him were surely with us and rejoiced to see our day of harvest among the outcastes of the South; the Visible and the Invisible seemed so one that no melancholy overtook me, though as far as my personal share in the work is concerned I see "the golden evening brightening in the west." I looked long on that moving sight of many faces, villagers and teachers gathered from towns and hamlets far and near, realizing it is probably the last time I shall see a vast Telugu assembly. Many things are "last time" now.

In the evening I went for a little walk in the fields behind the mission bungalows. Some Mohammedan tombs offered seats; after these days, which for all the joy they held were a little fatiguing, the blessed quiet was welcome. Round me were *cholum* fields almost ripe for harvest; the tall stalks with their curved shining leaf-blades stood motionless; not a breath of wind was stirring. Cloudy and grey the sky hung above, the mountains showing misty and blue in the distance. In my immediate vicinity desolation and neglect reigned; for prickly pear and brambles overran the spaces between the tombs—the nameless tombs.

A great hush and stillness lay over the country stretching as far as eye could see ripe unto harvest. I looked at it with prayer and love, "Good-bye, good-bye. Whoever you are who live in the little villages denoted by those clumps of tamarind- and margosa-trees, may you be blessed, and when you gather this harvest now ripening around you may more than daily bread come to you with this gift of God. I shall not come this way again; but I love you to the end, and if I could I would bless you; may a love and a blessing higher than mine remain with you always."

* * * * *

The quay of Bombay is gliding past—or can it be I who am gliding away from India? The figures of a dear colleague, and of Jewel brave to the last, are lost from sight, as the shore is left behind. But then, what is sight? "A very great deal," says a sorely grieving heart; but a voice trusted now for many years breaks in, "The things that are not seen are eternal."